ANTISEMITISM

A History Portrayed

ANNE FRANK FOUNDATION

Editors:
Janrense Boonstra
Hans Jansen
Joke Kniesmeyer

2nd revised edition

Colophon
Translation:
Jean Kramer-Updike
Design:
Martijn Luns GLV Amsterdam
Typesetting and printing:
Ten Brink Meppel bv

ISBN 90 12 08032 0

Acknowledgements

In 1976, the Anne Frank Foundation organized an exhibition titled *2000 Years of Antisemitism*. A few years ago the idea arose of focussing attention on this subject again, but this time in greater detail and with more illustrations.

One of the focal points of the Anne Frank Foundation is fighting prejudice against Jews in all of its manifestations. An exhibition in the Anne Frank House about the history of antisemitism and its expression, with a catalogue to accompany it, are one means of doing so.

We would like to express our deep gratitude to Dr. Hans Jansen, who wrote most of the text in this catalogue. He was also closely associated with the planning and realization of the exhibition.

Joke Kniesmeyer and Janrense Boonstra from the Anne Frank Foundation worked on this project. The latter was also the chief editor of the catalogue as well as the exhibition. Vera Ebels Dolanová was responsible for a great part of the research. Dienke Hondius should also be mentioned here for her invaluable help in collecting illustrations.

The production of the catalogue was carried out by the SDU, which led to a good, stimulating cooperation. The SDU assigned the lay-out of the catalogue to Martijn Luns, who, with the same expertise, designed the exhibition. The exhibition and catalogue were made possible partly with financial support of the Ministries of O&W and WVC. A donation was also received from the Etty Hillesum Foundation. Many people and institutions contributed illustrations, some with little or no charge for the copyright. For this help, we would like to thank all those concerned.

Anne Frank Foundation
Amsterdam

CONTENTS

'To our great horror and regret we hear that the attitude of a great many people towards us Jews has changed. We hear that there is anti-semitism now in circles that never thought of it before. ...Oh, it is sad, very sad, that once more, for the umpteenth time, the old truth is confirmed: "What one *Christian* does is his own responsibility, what one *Jew* does is thrown back at all Jews."*

Anne Frank, May 22, 1944.

Introduction

The concept antisemitism refers to ideas and actions directed against Jews and Judaism. Antisemitism is currently associated with the Nazi murder of six million Jews between 1933 and 1945. Compared to this, everything that preceded it seems to pale in comparison, but antisemitism has had a long history.

Demonstrations of hatred against Jews can be traced from the first centuries of the Christian era. The rise and expansion of Christianity has played the most important role. In the Middle Ages, social and economic sources of antisemitism also came into being. The transition to a new age under the Reformation and Counter Reformation brought no fundamental change in the attitude towards Jews. When the spirit of the Enlightenment blew across Europe in the eighteenth century, at first the tide seemed to have turned: one example of this was that during the French Revolution even Jews were granted equal civil rights. The nineteenth century, however, revealed a newly revived antisemitism. Quasi-scientific theories made the Jews out to be an inferior race. In addition, antisemitism became a political program.

This history over hundreds of years reached its depths in the Germany of Adolf Hitler: nearly all the Nazi measures against Jews had been conceived and put into practice earlier – with the exception of the *'final solution of the Jewish problem'*, as the Nazis cynically referred to the extermination.

After 1945, certainly in Western Europe, there was a general taboo on open antisemitism. This was not true of the Communist countries. A hostile attitude towards the Jewish population was characteristic of the Soviet Union and its satellites and was inspired, or at least tolerated by the government until well into the 'eighties. The Arab countries developed their own brand of antisemitism after the foundation of Israel in 1948 and under the influence of various wars. An important role is played by anti-Zionism, which denies the right of Israel to exist as a Jewish state. In the Western Europe of the 'eighties, there is a conspicuous explosion of violence against Jewish organizations and individuals.

Radical circles still try to deny or explain away Nazi crimes. This form of antisemitism has a strong effect on many people, but it is fortunately limited to a few small groups. Greater social alarm arises when attempts to master the difficult past take on such forms that one can safely call it repression.

Attention has been given to all the aspects mentioned above in this catalogue and in the exhibition of the same title. This is in the first place a history *in* pictures: an anti-Jewish language of images as it has developed over hundreds of years. It is apparent that while the manner of expression changes, if often only slightly, the themes have remained the same for centuries. In the second place, it is the history *of* an image: the image that the antisemite has created in his mind of *the Jew* with the help of the statements, texts, books, laws and treatises of influential thinkers and policy makers. In the third place, the results of these images, their creation and policy, are considered: anti-Jewish measures and explosions of violence. All in all, this is not a positive history. Cooperation between Jews and Christians or between Jews and Moslems, equal rights for a Jewish minority in a non-Jewish society, opposition to antisemitism: these and similar matters are not the subject here. This exhibition and catalogue concentrate on the most important developments and moments in the history of antisemitism. We do not claim that this coverage is exhaustive.

Although the exhibition and catalogue have the same basis and follow the same line, they overlap only partially. The introductory texts of the chapters are the basic texts of the exhibition. The text of the book is composed of a number of sections, in which specific aspects of the development of antisemitism are covered in more detail.

The Anne Frank Foundation hopes that through this display of pictures and the literal quotations of statements and texts, current forms of antisemitism can be recognized more readily. In our opinion, fighting antisemitism is not only the responsibility of the government and organizations; it is everyone's responsibility.

The content of the exhibition and catalogue are meant to help achieve this goal.

Chapter 1

The Roman Age and early Christianity

In the Roman Empire before Christianity there were more than four million Jews, about seven per cent of the total population. They were the only people who believed in one God. Writers of antiquity frequently blamed the Jews for clinging to their own customs and not honoring the *official* gods.

Jealousy can have played a role in this:
because Judaism was appealing. The encouragement by the state of antisemitism was scarcely known in the Roman Empire during this period.

The spread of Christianity, that had broken off from Judaism, began via the Jewish communities. Rivalry developed between the two almost at once. The Christians saw the destruction of the Jewish Temple in Jerusalem in the year 70 as a divine punishment for the rejection of Jesus as the Messiah. But the dividing lines between Judaism and Christianity were still vague.

1. Relief from the Arch of Titus in Rome, erected to celebrate the victory over the Jews. Triumphal procession through Rome with the spoils, including a seven-branched candelabrum, *menorah*.

Antisemitism in Antiquity

Antisemitism in Antiquity was fundamentally religious. In classical writings it is apparent that the religious
way of life of the Jews was a source of
irritation. The exclusive worship of
the God of the Jewish people meant
the refusal to participate in the cult of
other gods. That led to accusations of
atheism. The Jews were viewed by the
Roman writers in particular as a god-
less people, and one hated by the gods.
What is more, they were said to have
made a tradition of this hatred with
all others; it had become a law for
them not to break bread with non-
Jews. They were accused of showing
the way only to Jews, and when asked

2. Romain coin, minted to
commemorate the victory
over the Jews. The inscription reads: *Judaea capta*
(Judea conquered).

where water could be found, they
would only lead Jews to a well.

One of the antisemitic themes heard
repeatedly was that Jews worshipped
the donkey, and therefore a donkey's

head was placed in their temple. The
following story was often told, too: the
Jews were originally lepers driven out
of Egypt. Many Roman writers believed that an epidemic had broken
out in Egypt which disfigured people's
bodies. When King Bocchoris consulted the oracle of Ammon to request
a cure, he was ordered to purify his
kingdom and to deport the Jews. Two
Greek writers circulated the legend of
ritual murder: Jews were said to cap-
ture a Greek every year, fatten him
up in the temple, and finally murder
him for a ceremonial purpose. The
first pogrom in Jewish history, and

3. Christianity begins to spread: the ruins of a small Christian house-chapel near those of a large synagogue in the Roman city, Dura-Europos (on the Euphrates).

explosion of anti-Jewish violence, took place in Alexandria in 38 a.d. The arrival of Herod Agrippa was the direct provocation for it. Jews ridiculed him by dressing a vagrant, Carabas, well-known and simpleminded, like a king and honoring him enthusiastically. Because the governor, Flaccus, understood the danger in ridiculing a friend of the Emperor's, he declared the Jews to be foreigners and intruders. The city's inhabitants assumed that they could do as they liked to the Jews. The Jews, living scattered around the city, were now driven together in one section. They were forced to leave their homes and shops, which were plundered. Men, women and children were dragged through the streets, beaten to death and thrown onto bonfires.

The Beginning of Christian Communities

It is not surprising that the first Christians lived within Jewish society. After all, Jesus was a Jew who belonged to a small tribe without political power living on the border of the Roman Empire. He worked under and for Jews. His mother, Maria, his father, Joseph, his family and his followers were Jews. His name was Jewish as were his bible, his worship service and his prayers. Under the circumstances, he could not consider preaching to heathens. His message only applied to the Jewish people.

The first Christians followed a Jewish way of life. Their bible was the Hebrew bible. The texts of the New Testament were added to the Hebrew bible. The Gospel Jesus preached was based entirely on the assumptions of the Law and the Prophets. The first Christians were completely convinced that Jesus had never rejected the Jewish people and they continued to remember what their preacher had said in his sermon on the mount: '*Think not that I am come to destroy the Law, or the Prophets: I am not come to destroy but to fulfill. For verily I say unto you, till heaven and earth pass, one jot or one tittle shall in no wise pass from the law, till all be fulfilled.*' (Matthew 5: 17-18)

The process of separation from Jewish society had its spiritual foundation in the confession that Jesus was the Messiah of Israel. The schism was precipitated by the establishment of communities by non-Jews who did not conform to the laws of Moses. The

4. Part of the Western Wall (the so-called Wailing Wall), the last remains of the Temple in Jerusalem

non-Jewish Christians soon formed an overwhelming majority. After a few decades, the separation became final when the Temple was destroyed in Jerusalem in the year 70, and services there came to an end. The Church, which stemmed from Jews, was finally altered into a church of non-Jews.

At the time, the Jews, who did not accept Jesus as the Messiah of Israel, were hostile to the young Church. Towards the end of the first century, the Jewish-Christians were excluded from Jewish society, and the schism had become a fact.

'... suffered under Pontius Pilate'

At the time the four Gospels were edited in their final form, a process had begun, intended to declare Pontius Pilate, the Roman governor, innocent of the crucifixion of Jesus. How can we explain this? That Jesus was Jewish and that he had been crucified by the Romans were two large stumbling-blocks for the spread of Christianity in the Roman Empire. After the persecution of the Christians under Nero and the bloody repression of the Jewish rebellion in Palestine – during which the Temple in Jerusalem also fell victim – the policy of the Church was aimed at winning the Roman emperors' tolerance for the Christian religion. It was therefore vital that in the Gospels, Rome's responsibility for the crucifixion should be limited and the guilt of the Jews be made as great as possible. The Gospels were edited so that all the Romans were presented sympathetically, and Pontius Pilate especially, who had to appear as innocent as a lamb. On the other hand, the unanimity of all four Gospels is conspicuous in assuming the Jews to be guilty for the death of Jesus.

If Jews had played a crucial role in passing sentence on or executing Jesus, the bishops would without doubt have included such convincing evidence in the *Nicene Creed* of 381.

5. Paul arguing with the Jews, a traditional Christian portrayal of the New versus the Old Testament.
ENAMEL PANEL. 11TH CENT.

But, on the contrary, this Creed states that Jesus '...*suffered under Pontius Pilate.*' Jesus did not suffer *under Kajafas*, nor *under the Pharisees*, nor *under the Jews*. In a Coptic translation of a Christian text from the second century, only Pontius Pilate is held responsible for the crucifixion of Jesus. Finally, Tacitus, writing in the second decade of the second century, said in his Annals: '*Christ was executed during the reign of Emperor Tiberius by his procurator Pontius Pilate.*'

Melito of Sardis

In the second century, Melito, Bishop of Sardis in Asia Minor, was the first to formulate the myth of the murder of God. In an Easter sermon that has become famous, he said: *'Israel (The Jewish People), what have you done? Have you not read the text from the Scriptures? 'Shed no innocent blood to your own destruction.' 'I have verily killed the Lord,' the Jewish People answer. The Lord must*

6. The obstinacy of the Jews as Christians saw it: their hands over their ears, they refuse to listen to the Christian Gospel.
ILLUSTRATION FROM A MANUSCRIPT IN THE MONASTERY OF MONTE CASSINO. 1023.

suffer but not through you. He must be executed, but not under your jurisdiction. For him, you prepared sharp nails and false witnesses, chains and floggings, vinegar and gall, the sword and misery, as for a murderer. And thus you killed the Lord on the great Holy Day. Oh, Israel, you did not know that this was God's firstborn son. Israel, you who broke the Law, why did you commit this injustice, plunging your Lord into unheard of torment: your Lord, who formed you, who created you, who honored you, who called you Israel (God's warrior). You raised your voices against God, He before whom the peoples prostrated themselves, whom the uncircumcised admired, for whom even Pilate washed his hands, you killed him on the great Holy Day (Jewish Passover). You killed the Lord in the middle of Jerusalem. Hear, all generations of the peoples, and see: an unheard of murder was committed in the middle of Jerusalem, the city of the Law. And who was murdered? He who nailed down the earth, He who made fast the heaven, He was himself nailed down. He who created the universe was himself nailed

to the wood. The Lord was killed. God was murdered. The King of Israel was eliminated by Jewish hands. Oh, this unheard of murder! Oh, this unheard of injustice!'

In 1957, Joseph Weill, a professor in Strasbourg, wrote about this accusation of the murder of God, so endlessly repeated: *'Since two thousand years ago up to the present day, this accusation has sorely oppressed every individual Jew and every generation of Jews, like unbearable and unavoidable, unmerciful and inhuman fate.'*

Explanation of the Text: 'Then answered all the people and said, His blood be on us, and on our children.' (Matthew 27:25)

In the third century, the Greek patriarch, Origines of Alexandria, wrote in his commentary on the Gospel according to Matthew: *'And Pilate washed his hands, but the Jews did not want to purify themselves through the blood of Christ, but let it flow over them as revenge when they spoke: 'His blood be on us, and on our children!' They are therefore not only guilty of the blood of the prophets, but also of the blood of Christ. Therefore they hear God say to them 'When you reach out your hands, I shall hide my face from you, because your hands are full of blood.' Therefore they let Christ's blood flow not only over the Jews who were contemporaries of Jesus, but also over all the generations of Jews to come until the end of time.'*

Through the centuries, hundreds of prominent thinkers among bishops and theologians have interpreted this infamous text in the same way, pleading the great authority of Origines.

In 1909, the Jewish scholar, Montefiore, said of this text in his commentary on the Gospels: *'A frightful text. A horrifying concoction. Notice the bitter hatred that moves the evangelist to write "the whole nation". The whole nation was expected to be present. In this way, all*

the shameful atrocities that Christianity
and the Church as accessory have committed against Jews were accepted by the Jews
as having been brought on by themselves.
That is one of the sentences which has been
responsible for oceans of human blood and
an endless stream of misery and desolation.'

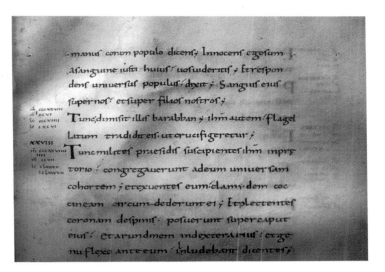

7. Section of the New
Testament, Matthew 27/25
with the text: 'His blood be
on us, and on our children'.
PARCHMENT. 10TH CENT.

8. Accusation of God's
murder: Jews (with me-
dieval hats for Jews) nailing
Jesus to the Cross.
FRESCO. LANDAU. C. 1500.

Chapter 2

Policy of the Church Fathers and the Early Middle Ages

When Christianity became the most important religion of the Roman Empire in 313, it brought an end to the period of relative tolerance. The church fathers opposed the Jews with unknown fervour; they accused them of having murdered God and of being the children of the devil.

Through words and images, the Christians had to be made aware that the Christian Church (Ecclesia) had triumphed over the Jewish Synagogue.

All kinds of measures were taken by the spiritual and secular rulers to prevent Christians and Jews from mingling. For this purpose, the religious and social-economic rights of Jews were increasingly restricted. In 534, Emperor Justinian had anti-Jewish regulations written into the Roman code of law. This *Justinian Code* has had a great influence for centuries.

1. Bishop Ambrose of Milan, a Church Father of the 4th century. He opposed the reconstruction of a synagogue burned down by Christians, '... so that no place would exist where God was denied'.
MOSAIC IN THE ST. AMBROGIO, MILAN.

2. The Old Testament being buried with the Tables of the Law by Christ and the four Evangelists.
FRENCH BIBLE MINIATURE. C. 1410.

Emperor Constantine and the Jews

The decisive moment for the Church came in 313, when, under Emperor Constantine, Christianity became the official religion. The Edict of Milan officially guaranteed the Church unlimited freedom of religion for the first time. But the religious freedom announced by Constantine proved not to apply to Jews. He prescribed that if a Jewish community dared to take in a heathen, a fiery death would be the punishment. The same sentence would be passed on anyone preventing a Jew from becoming a Christian. He also proclaimed that all the slaves subjected to ritual circumcision by their owners would be freed. Constantine decreed new guidelines for Jewish visits to Jerusalem. The old ones dated from Hadrian, and had been in effect for almost two hundred years. Jerusalem became a forbidden city for the Jews. The regulation was very strict and was directed not only at Jews but also at Jewish Christians. Violation of this law was punishable by death. Constantine did, however, permit Jews to make a pilgrimage to Jerusalem once a year on 9 ab, the anniversary of the destruction of the Temple in 70. On that day they were also allowed to enter Jerusalem together to express their grief. In the Emperor's opinion, it could do no harm to remind the Jews annually of Roman supremacy. Early in his reign Constantine was aware of the bishops' effort to isolate the Jews as much as possible.

3. John Crysostom, a Church Father of the 4th century. His antisemitic sermons had a great influence for centuries.
MOSAIC IN THE PALACE CHAPEL IN PALERMO. C. 1148.

John Chrysostom

John Crysostom was the most eloquent Greek church father, the court preacher to the Bishop of Antioch, in what is now known as Syria. In Antioch, many Christians sympathized with the Synagogue: they often visited the services there on the Sabbath and on other holidays, they went to Jewish doctors, and not infrequently, they turned to Jewish courts. The clergy of the city regarded these developments as a great danger to the Church. In previous centuries, church politics were directed at changing or even eliminating everything that recalled Judaism. The bishop, therefore, instructed his court preacher to haul them over the coals. In one of his eight notorious sermons, he said: *'Do not let it surprise you that I have called the Jews disastrous. Because they are really*

 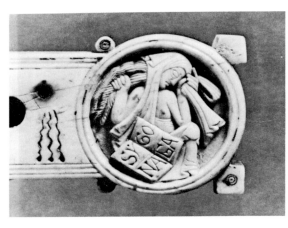

4. Ivory medallions showing Church and Synagogue. The Synagogue is portrayed as a blind old woman, with bared breast, pulling the hair out of her head.
GUNHILDE CROSS. 11TH CENT.

disastrous and miserable. They who have so fervently rejected and thrown away the many good things heaven has put into their hands. They have known the prophets from childhood on and have crucified the one they prophesized about. They who were called to be sons have descended to the race of dogs. Unreasoning animals, when they enjoy mangers that are full and grow fat, become more difficult and unmanageable, and will not tolerate a yoke or reins, or the driver's hand. And so with the nation of Jews: because they have turned to the most extreme evil, they have become restive and have not accepted the yoke of Christ or been harnessed to the plough of his teachings. Such unreasoning animals are suited for slaughter, because they are not suited for work. The Jews have had to experience that: because they showed themselves useless for work, they have become suitable for slaughter. I know that many persons respect the Jews, and regard their life as honorable. I hasten, therefore, to pluck out this depraved bias by the roots. I have said that the synagogue is not better than the theatre. Indeed, the synagogue is not only a brothel and a theatre, but also a den for robbers and a shelter for wild beasts. And not only for wild beasts, but even for impure wild beasts.'

Immediately after his death in 407, his eight anti-Jewish sermons (treatises) were circulated through the entire Church, and before long, they were translated into Latin, Syrian, Russian and other languages. Frag-ments of these sermons were included in the *Byzantine Liturgy for the Holy Week*.

Augustine

Augustine became bishop of the small coastal town, Hippo, in what is now Tunesia, in 396. His influence on theological thought has remained so great that he can only be compared to the Apostle Paul.

Augustine's view of the Jews' place in Christian society was completely original. According to him, after the destruction of Jerusalem and the Temple, the Jews had to fulfill a twofold service for the Church. In the first place: '*... the degradation of the Jews all over the world (serves) as a contrast to the beauty of the form of the Church.*' In this way the Jews were used as an example to warn the Church.

In the second place, the Synagogue had to bear witness throughout the world to the truth of the Church as well as to her own deceit. The Synagogue had fortunately taken all its writings along, which included pre-dictions about Christ and the Church. These writings had foretold the terrible punishment of the Jews for their crimes. Anyone who doubted the truth of the Church, could there-fore turn to the Synagogue to allay his doubts. The Synagogue survived the catastrophe of the year 70 for no other reason than to enable the Church to survive in the world. For this reason, the Synagogue had to remain in existence. Jews had to continue to come together in their synagogues, not for their own salvation, but for the salvation of the Christians. The Jews gathered like the blind to light the way to eternal life with their writings for Christians, having forfeited it themselves. Because Jews were allowed to survive as slaves of the Church, however, they could not be killed.

Theodosian Code

In 438, the *Theodosian Code* was published by Emperor Theodosius II. All the laws formulated between 213 and 437 were brought together in one book of law. The anti-Jewish laws were included in chapters 8 and 9 of part XVI. Whoever reads these laws gets an idea of the social, economic and political degradation of the Jews in that Christian society. The Jewish religion was described as being a depraved sect, a criminal religion, an infectious disease, and Christians had to be protected against it by forbidding every form of human association. While the Jewish religion was still a 'legitimate religion', every attempt was made to make the Jewish religion die out. The church leaders followed a policy that isolated the Jews in Christian society more and more fatally. There was still no persecution, but the Jewish religion was described in the laws as an infectious disease which led to death.

Justinian Code

In 534, the famous *Corpus Iuris Civilis* appeared, in which Emperor Justinian had Roman law codified. There is no other work in antiquity that has had so great an influence on European history. All the laws concerning the Jewish religion and its followers were set down in the *Justinian Code*, the third section of the book. Its discriminating regulations were later adopted by practically all the lawbooks of European states. The *Justinian Code* degraded the Jew to second-class citizenship. From then on, the Jewish religion was no longer a legitimate

5. Mediaeval copy of the Justinian Code.

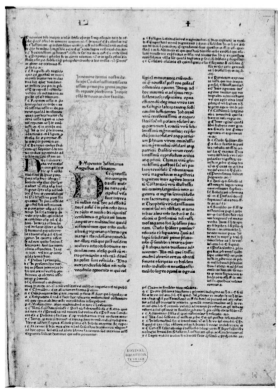

6. Depictions of Church and Synagogue. The blindfolded Synagogue with a broken staff on a donkey; the crown is falling from the head that is pierced from above.
STAINED GLASS WINDOW. WERBEN, GERMANY.

The Toledo Synods

In the seventh century, numerous synods were held in Toledo, then capitol of Spain, which enacted anti-Jewish measures. In the synod held in 694, the bishops prescribed that at age seven, Jewish children of both sexes were forbidden to go on living with their parents or to maintain any contact with them. The children were given to gentlemen, who were responsible for their upbringing with reliable Christians.

This severe policy stemmed from the views the Toledo archbishops developed about the Jews in this period. Julian of Toledo said: *'Just as a cancer tumor attacks the healthy parts of the body, Jews with their lunatic claims affect the spiritual health of Christians.'* And Ildefons of Toledo wrote: *'I believe that with God's help I have impaled and struck down the enemy as well as possible, so that, powerless and dead, he now lies on the ground. There the Jew lies, weak, deadly pale, having bled to death, choked with fear. He died when he was hurled to the ground. There is no longer any hope that the breath of life will return and he will come back to life. Now he only has to exhale his belief. I shall not rest until he lies completely crushed under my feet, because I want to prevent that even a tiny worm of unbelief remains alive on his corpse, and not a single moth — of any sort at all — shall grow in the cadaver of the scandalous criminal and then appear, and finally, that not a single sort of worm shall come into being from the decaying slime of the foul Godlessness and shall creep out of the cadaver.'*

one. To paraphrase a few regulations of this Code:
- anyone who tempts a Christian to turn his back on his religion and then converts him to Judaism will lose all his possessions and be punished by death;
- sexual relations between Jews and Christians are forbidden under threat of severe punishment;
- if Jews dare to circumcise Christians, they will lose all their possessions and will be banished for life;
- Jews may no longer claim any public office they have held;
- anyone daring to build a new synagogue will be fined fifty pounds of gold, will have his entire fortune confiscated, and will be punished by death.

The successors to Emperor Justinian, with the support of the bishops and monks, continually referred to the *Justinian Code* in their anti-Jewish policies.

Jews and Christians in Early Islam

In the seventh century Mohammed developed an Arabian variation of monotheism. Mohammed considered himself the last prophet after Jesus and saw in Islam the perfecting and crowning of Judaism and Christianity. He tolerated no unbelievers: in other words, those who refused to convert to Islam. The statement passed down from Mohammed: *'The earth belongs to Allah and his Prophet'*, is a foundation of Islam. When the Jews in Medina rejected his views, he declared *jihad*, holy war on them. He had the men of the Jewish community in Medina killed after all but one refused to convert, and he had the women and children carried off as slaves. According to the concept of jihad, the world is divided in *dar al-Islam*, the Islam domain where Islamic law applies, and the illegitimate *dar al-Harb*, conquered by unbelievers, the domain of war. The ethics and code of conduct which apply within the *dar al-Islam* are not applicable to the inhabitants of the *dar al-Harb*.

During the Islamic conquest in Arabia, North Africa, Asia Minor and Spain, the heathen population was killed, driven out or converted by force. Christians and Jews, *people of the Book* (the Gospels and the Torah) were subjected to the rules of the *dhimma*: in return for a large sum of money for protection and special taxes, they were allowed to live in the world of Islam in degradation and insecurity.

Mohammed attributed the Jews' refusal to accept him as the true prophet of God to what he saw as their vicious obstinacy, that had moved them to falsify and distort their own holy books which he thought foretold his arrival as a prophet. We feel his embitterment in various passages of

the Koran: *'Thou wilt surely find that the strongest in enmity against those who believe are the Jews and the idolators; and thou wilt find the nearest in love to those who believe to be those who say, "We are Christians".'* (Sura V, v. 85) The justification of Mohammed's policy towards the Jews is also laid down by the Koran: *'Fight – such men as practice not the religion of truth, being of those who*

7. Two statues portraying Church and Synagogue: the blindfolded Synagogue holding a broken staff and the Tables of the Law. Such statues appear in many medieval cathedrals.
SOUTHERN FACADE OF STRASBOURG CATHEDRAL. 1230-1240.

8. Church and Synagogue: the Church with the lance is attacking the Synagogue, seated on a pig and identifiable by the hat for Jews. PULPIT. CATHEDRAL IN ERFURT. C. 1400.

have been given the Book – until they pay the tribute out of hand and have been humbled.' (Sura IX, v. 29)

Mohammed's accusations found their way in many different forms into written and oral Islamic tradition. '*A Jew will not be found alone with a Moslem without planning to kill him,'* wrote Amr Ibn ahr al-Jahiz in 869. The policy of *dhimma,* the status of subjugation, was developed in the course of the seventh century, and in about 720 it became canonized in the so-called Charter of Umar. The policy of Caliph Umar b. al-Khattab (634-644) was supplemented in the next centuries with detailed regulations about clothing, profession, and association between dhimmi and Moslems, which the dhimmi's had to follow or be put to death. According to texts that have been handed down, Umar b. al-Khattab gave provincial governors instructions to require the dhimmi's to shave off their hair, wear lead or iron seals around their necks, not to sit astride their mules and to bind distinctive girdles around their waists so they could be distinguished from the Moslems.

In 807, Caliph Haroen al-Rashid introduced separate living areas, *mellah,* and the wearing of a yellow badge.

In 850, Caliph al-Mutawakkil ordered the destruction of all the houses of worship built after the coming of Islam, and the confiscation of one tenth of the houses. All the large buildings had to be rebuilt into mosques. He gave orders to nail wooden devils on the doors of houses to distinguish them from those of Moslems.

Al-Jahiz, one of the early Arab authors, observed in the ninth century that the Moslems looked down on Jews more than on Christians; they thought the Jews were more deceitful and treacherous than Christians and therefore deserved more punishment. According to al-Jahiz, this attitude was determined by the low economic and social status of the Jews: '*... and the greater respect* (of the Christians) *by the masses and fondness for them by the community stems from the fact that there are among them secretaries to sultans and servants of the Kings and physicians of the nobility, and spice merchants and moneychangers. Among the Jews (on the other hand) there are only dyers or tanners or bloodletters or butchers or harness-makers. And when the masses saw this among the Jews and Christians, they assumed (the worth) of the Jewish religion among the other faiths to be as (degraded) as their occupations among the other occupations,* *and that their heresy is the greatest of all since they are the filthiest of the nations.'*

The Conflict between the Carolingians and the Church

Charlemagne and his successors thought that the Jews with their varied interests and skills were of great importance to international trade. The Carolingians therefore guaranteed the Jews their lives, their right to worship and their possessions. The Jews also obtained the right to engage in trade. Of course, they had to pay a tenth of their annual income in gratitude for the protection granted them. The Carolingian' friendly policy towards Jews brought down the fury of the Pope and bishops on their heads. Pope Stephen III wrote an angry letter to Bishop Aribert of Narbonne: *'Overwhelmed by concern and alarm, we received your message that the Jewish people, who remained unruly towards God and averse to our customs, have been given the same status as Christians on Christian ground. In cities and suburbs, they call hereditary goods which are not leased their property, on the basis of privileges given them. Christians work the Jewish vineyards and fields. Christian men and woman live with these traitors under one roof and defile their souls with blasphemous words day and night; these unfortunate wretches must humble themselves to those dogs every day, every hour, and accede to their every whim. Justice alone demands that the promises made to these traitors be declared invalid, so that the death of the crucified Savior will finally be avenged.'*

Bishop Agobart of Lyons wrote in a letter to the Emperor that the social isolation of Jews was necessary in Christian society. He cited numerous texts from the Old and New Testaments, the texts of church fathers and the acts of councils to convince him that Christians are instructed to hate Jews. He praised Ambrose, Bishop of Milan, because he had the courage to approve of setting fire to a synagogue. What would the pious Ambrose not have done, if he had seen that the Carolingian Emperors flaunted the church laws against Jews. Bishop Agobert praised the behavior of Hilary, Bishop of Poitiers, who judged Jews not even worthy of a greeting. Finally, he advised the Emperor to put an archivist to work to explain in detail what all the church fathers wrote about the Synagogue of Satan. This would be an important contribution to the preservation of the Christian belief.

9. The so-called *Living Cross*, with the Church and Synagogue on either side. An arm out of the cross pierces the Synagogue, seated on a goat.
FRESCO FROM THE SAN PETRINO. BOLOGNA. 1421.

Chapter 3

The Period of the Crusades

At the end of 1095, Pope Urban II summoned a crusade to liberate Jerusalem from the grip of Islam. In the summer of 1096, when the crusade got started, several thousand Jews were murdered in the lands along the Rhine, and their houses were plundered. *'Because why should we go off to attack the unbelievers in the Holy Land'*, the crusaders asked, *'and leave the unbelievers in our midst untouched?'* Although local bishops sometimes tried to prevent the massacres, the prospect of looting Jewish possessions without reprisal was too attractive.

The Pope and bishops determined in 1215 that Jewish clothing should be different from that of Christians – to avoid having any sexual relations with Jews out of ignorance. Various clothing regulations were proclaimed: the yellow badge or ring in France, for example, or the pointed Jewish hat in Germany. Only through conversion could these humiliating regulations be avoided.

1. Pope Urban summons the First Crusade in Clermont, France in 1095.

2. Two Jews, identifiable by their hats, being put to the sword. Bible illustration from the period of the crusaders' persecutions. FRANCE. C. 1250.

crusaders passed through cities where Jews lived on the way, they said to each other, as Salamon ben Simeon wrote: *'See, we cover great distances to seek the site of the Holy Grave and to avenge ourselves on the Moslems. And see, here among us live the Jews, who put the innocent Christ to death and crucified him. Let us first avenge ourselves on them and root them out of society, so the name Jew will no longer be mentioned.'*

3. Jews (with hats for Jews) burning in hell, surrounded by devils. FROM HORTUS DELICIARUM. GERMANY. 1175.

Christian Justification of the Crusades

In 1140, Salamon ben Simeon, the Jewish chronicle writer in Mainz, noted that crusaders said the following: *'He has said: "The day will come when my sons will avenge my blood." We are His sons and it is our duty to take revenge on you because of your rebellious and criminal behavior towards Him. You have never been thankful to God for the goodness He has given you. You have always acted deceitfully towards Him. That is why He has forgotten you, and does not love you, because you were a stubborn people. He has cast you out, he has shed his light on us and accepted us as his own.'* About the army commander, Godfrey of Bouillon, Salamon ben Simeon wrote: *'He has sworn the angry oath that he would only follow this way to avenge the Blood of his Savior by spilling the blood of the Jewish people and he would leave absolutely nothing of anyone calling himself a Jew. He also wanted to prevent Jews from fleeing to escape the bloodbath. He was filled with wrath against us.'* When the

Developments in Spain and North Africa

In the eleventh and twelfth centuries, Jews fell victim to the wars between Christianity and Islam to reconquer Spain and the Middle East. At the beginning of the eleventh century, the Christians tried to exploit the delicate position of the Arab rulers, who were divided amongst themselves, to reconquer Spain. But the Christian armies were defeated by the Almoravid, Islamic warriors, who subjected the country to a reign of terror. Under the Almoravid Dynasty the persecution of Jews and Christians was especially violent. In 1037, more than six thousand Jews were murdered in the Moroccan city, Fez. In 1066, five thousand Jews were killed in Granada.

The Almohad Dynasty carried out a policy of enforced conversions. When, in 1146, they conquered Sijilmasa and gave Jews the choice between conversion and death, a hundred and fifty Jews prefered death.

Abu-Jusuf al-Mansur, who reigned from 1184 to 1198, harbored suspicion about the sincerity of the Jews' conversion to Islam. He introduced clothing regulations to make both the converted Jews and the unconverted ones recognizable at all times. They had to wear dark blue clothes with sleeves down to their feet, and a hat in the shape of a saddle. Al-Mansur declared that the same regulations applied to those Jews who had converted under his predecessors, and to their descendants.

In justification of the persecution of Jews, the thirteenth century Syrian Arab writer, Abd al-Rahim al-Jawbari wrote: '*It is known that this group is the most cursed of all God's creation, the most evil-natured, and the most deeply rooted in infidelity and accursedness. They are the most evil intentioned of mankind in their deeds, even though they are the most ostentatious in humility and self-abasement... When they manage to be alone with a man, they bring him to destruction, they introduce by trickery a stupefying drug into his food, and then they kill him.*'

Clothing Regulations for Jews

Yellow badges appeared in various shapes from 1215 on, but the round shape remained predominant.

Different interpretations existed to explain this round shape. A frequent explanation was the following: the wafer or Host of Holy Mass, the symbol of the body of Christ, was round. The round shape reminded Christians of the Jews' guilt in crucifying Jesus, the son of God. The *yellow badge* thus became a sign for the Jews as murderers of God. A second explanation was: a coin was round as was the zero that increased every number. The Christians of the Middle Ages thus saw the sign of the Jew as usurer in the round *yellow badge*.

The symbolism of colors was very pronounced in the Middle Ages. Women guilty of *racial disgrace*, having sexual relations with Jews, were dragged through the streets to their execution, wearing a yellow hat. The *yellow badge* the Jews were forced to wear after the Fourth Lateran Council foreshadowed another 'solution' to the Jewish problem. Stigmatization aided the process of isolating and eliminating the Jews in society.

4. Early English caricature of a Jew: 'Aaron, son of the devil.' The obligatory badge on his tunic with the Tables of the Law.
ESSEX, ENGLAND. 1277.

5. The form of the hat imposed on Jews by law in Frankfurt.
ENGRAVING. 15TH CENT.

6. A Jewish family as portrayed in an Italian altar piece.
SANT' ANDREA. MANTUA. 14TH CENT.

Burning of Hebrew Literature

In his bull of June 19, 1239, Pope Gregory IX ordered the confiscation of all copies of the Talmud (the teachings and practice of Judaism). In France, Dominicans carried out this order on the first Sabbath of Lent by raiding the synagogues and removing all the Hebrew literature. In 1242, twenty-four horse-pulled carts clattered through the streets of Paris loaded with Hebrew literature. All the Jewish texts were consigned to the flames of a bonfire in a city square.

For Jews, the burning of their texts was almost on a par with the physical pain their companions suffered. Despite being on the fringes of society, the Jews were extremely active intellectually: they wrote thousands of books on philosophy and theological questions, they were familiar with the many extensive books of the Talmud and wrote commentaries about them. They steadfastly defied their opponents. They could be assaulted and beaten to death, but they never abandoned their deepest convictions. The pope and bishops knew that their study of the Talmud renewed their strength to resist and that is why they dried up the well. Their attack on the Talmud was a direct attack on the religion of the Jewish people and on the existence of the Jews themselves.

The attack Pope Gregory IX made on Hebrew literature was not incidental, for many of his successors continued his policy. In 1322, for example, Pope John XXII ordered all copies of the Talmud to be burned in triumph on the eve of the Jewish Pesach (Passover). The burning of Hebrew literature was almost always followed by an attack on the Jews themselves. Five hundred years later, the German poet Heine wrote: *'Where books are burned, eventually people are also burned.'*

1. Three of the six tableaus from an Italian predella of the so-called desecration of the Host. a) A Jewish pawnbroker buying a stolen Host. b) The Jewish family looking shocked at the blood flowing from the burned Host, while soldiers are breaking in. c) The entire family burned at the stake.
PANEL BY PAOLO UCCELLO. C. 1465.

Anti-Jewish Myths and Legends

In the Middle Ages, anti-Jewish accusations assumed absurd proportions.

For instance, Jews were said to murder Christian children to use their blood in preparing Pesach-matzes.

Such charges usually resulted in flourishing pilgrim resorts for the Church on one side,.and on the other, the murder or expulsion of the Jewish community. That was also true of the charges of desecrating the sacred wafer, the Host. In 1215, the Pope proclaimed the dogma that the Host was the actual body of Christ. The accusation was that in desecrating the Host, the Jews were killing Jesus again and again. There were numerous legends about how the stolen Host was saved by all kinds of miracles. In the middle of the fourteenth century, a plague epidemic broke out in Europe, which killed approximately one-third of the population. It was then unknown how the illness spread, but the story circulated that the Jews had poisoned the wells. Thousands of Jews were murdered on this charge in, among other places, Basel, Strasbourg, Mainz, Worms and Cologne.

Mass expulsions of Jews often marked the end of a campaign of hatred.

2. Three of a series of six Spanish scenes about a Jew who steals an image of the Virgin Mary. Two devils dragging him away to hell. FROM THE HYMNBOOK *LAS CANTIGAS DE SANTA MARIA.* 13TH CENT.

3. The story of the ritual murder of Simon of Trent in 1475, later declared a saint. This anti-Jewish accusation was maintained by the Church until about 1950.
GERMAN WOODCUT. 1493.

Legend of the Ritual Murder

In the twelfth century, the Jews were first accused of ritual murder. Two incidents are cited here. The oldest known legend of ritual murder dates from 1144. On Good Friday, Jews were said to have tortured, hung and then burned William of Norwich. The most famous accusation of ritual murder took place in Trent in northern Italy: on Maundy Thursday, 1475, Simon, the son of a tanner and barely three years old, disappeared. A monk, Bernardino Feltre, and Bishop Hinderbach accused the Jews of torturing, killing and throwing Simon's body into the water.

In this first stage of the legend's development, it was said that Jews murdered a Christian child during the Holy Week, and especially on Good Friday, as if to crucify Jesus once again. What they had done to Jesus

before, they would now do to his followers.

In the second stage, it was said that Jews murdered the children of Christian parents in connection with the celebration of their Passover. Jews were said to need Christian blood for preparing the unleavened bread and for mixing with wine. In addition, a third version appeared, sometimes in relation to the previous two, but also independently.

Jews were said to need Christian blood for the practice of magic. Because the blood of children was virginal and innocent, it would also be the most potent. Aside from its use for sorcery, it would also serve medicinal purposes: against haemorrhoids, against the so-called *stink of Jews*, for the relief of pain during circumcision, for increasing fertility and for many other purposes.

The charge of ritual murder would continue until long into the twentieth century.

Legend of the Desecration of the Host

From the Middle Ages, the legend has been told that Jews stole the Hosts from churches and pierced them with knives and awls to crucify the body of Jesus again. This legend arose in a period when Christians no longer took it for granted that the priest's words during mass mysteriously changed the bread into the body of Christ. Doubt and disbelief about this transsubstantiation had to be conquered by stories of miracles. Legends relating all kinds of miracles that happened after the desecration of the Host had to reconfirm this church dogma. The legend of the violation of the Host – which was usually originated by the clergy – also served to legitimize the persecution of Jews. People in the Middle Ages were sure that Jews were constantly trying to crucify Jesus again. So what accusation could have been more obvious? In 1390, an anonymous German monk wrote the following concerning the violation of a Host in Deggendorf:

'In the year 1337 the body of the Lord that had been tortured by the Jews was found in Deggendorf. Therefore the Jews were burned in the year 1338.'

Pamphlet about a desecration of a Host. Jews, recognized by the badges on their clothing, buy the stolen Host and pierce it with a sword (above right). Angels and doves fly out of the stove where the Host is burned. The Jews are captured, tortured and executed. A church is raised on the site of the synagogue. PASSAU, BAVARIA. 1478.

Legend of the Poisoning of the Wells

The accusation that the Jews had poisoned all the wells and springs to exterminate the Christians, their sworn enemies, had terrible consequences. This absurd charge was believed because the European masses had heard so much about Jews as murderers of God, who committed ritual murders and desecrated the Host. In Switzerland and Germany, primarily, Jews were subjected to torture on the rack, to the axe of the executioner, or to a fiery death on the bonfire, as if all Jews had to be swept from the surface of the earth.

Sixty large Jewish communities and one hundred and fifty smaller ones across all of Western Europe were burnt down to the ground and every single occupant was killed. After the slaughter of all the Jews in Zwolle in 1349, the burgomaster declared: *'They have been killed for the love of God with fire and the sword.'*

In the *Limburger Chronicle* these mass slaughters of Jews were justified as fulfilling the curse that the Jews had called down on themselves and their descendants on Good Friday: *'His blood be on us, and on our children.'* (Matthew 27/25). It was said that the Jews had only themselves to blame that they were put to death in this way.

But other motives played an important role in the persecution of Jews in 1348-1349. The *Constance World Chronicle* wrote that Christians persecuted and burned Jews to death to acquire their possessions, and the *Strasbourger Chronicle* noted: *'Their jingling coins formed the poison that killed the Jews'*.

5. King Philip August driving the Jews, wearing the yellow badges, out of France in 1182.
MINIATURE IN A FRENCH CHRONICLE. 1321.

6. The Jews, accused of causing the plague, being burned at the stake.
ILLUSTRATION FROM A FLEMISH CHRONICLE. 1349.

7. Portrayals of the so-called *Jewish swine* appear for centuries, and are especially offensive because Jews consider the pig impure. This German pamphlet of 1678 repeats the accusation of ritual murder and was sold in front of the entrance to the ghetto in Frankfurt.

Chapter 5

Economic Sources of Antisemitism

In the last half of the Middle Ages, an increasing number of occupational groups formed guilds. Membership in a guild was limited to Christians, and only members of guilds were allowed to practice a craft. Jews were thus excluded from more and more occupations. The one alternative to trading in secondhand goods permitted was lending money at a rate of interest. For Christians this was explicitly forbidden by the Church as a sin. The unstable political and economic situation made interest rates high.

This situation, the result of anti-Jewish measures, became the source of a new and tenacious antisemitic stereotype: the Jew as a greedy moneylender.

Jews could buy protection from secular lords – for a great deal of money! – but they were never certain of their position. It was common for powerful persons who were in debt to Jews to banish them from the city or the country. Various anti-Jewish attitudes of economic or religious origin became deeply anchored in the thinking of the Christian world towards the end of the Middle Ages, and the result was a fundamentally anti-Jewish attitude.

1. The bloodmoney: the Pharisee who is paying Judas for his betrayal, wearing a hat for Jews.
BIBLE ILLUSTRATION, AUSTRIA. 14TH CENT.

2. A Jewish banker and a German farmer.
WOODCUT FROM AUGSBURG 1531.

3. Anti-Jewish measures were justified by referring to the Bible: Jesus drove the moneylenders – with the medieval hats for Jews - from the Temple.
GERMAN STAINED GLASS WINDOW.

4. 'Day and night the Jew thinks how to ruin the Christians'. The Jew as Pickpocket, Merchant and Usurer.
GERMAN PAMPHLET. 15TH CENT.

5. A cartoon about Josel van Rosheim, a leading figure in the Jewish community in the Alsace, worshipping the Golden Calf. It was obvious to the medieval viewer: gold was the god of the Jews.
EARLY 16TH CENT.

'Kammerknechtschaft': Jews as Serfs of the Sovereign

In the Middle Ages, the doctrine of the *Kammerknechtschaft* of the Jews was developed. This doctrine held that Jews and all of their possessions were the property of the sovereign.

The religious view that the Jews were serfs of the Church (in that they had to bear witness to the truth of the Church and the deceit of the Synagogue) was thus translated into secular terms.

This was related to another development: after anti-Jewish outbursts of violence which followed the first crusade and the charges, brought against them of ritual murder, the Jews gradually lost the right to carry a weapon. In the Middle Ages, anyone without this right was not free, he was a 'serf' and dependant on the sovereign for his protection. The sovereign demanded the right to make the Jews pay a 'poll-tax' for their protection. The sovereign often granted bishops, counts and cities the privilege of demanding money from Jews and other privileges, such as that of charging tolls. These privileges could be leased, traded, given away or inherited.

Spiritual leaders supported this development because the theological doctrine of the eternal bondage of Jews was adopted by secular law. In the official canons of the Church, the *Corpus Iuris Canonici*, this doctrine was laid down in 1234 as follows: *'Christian piety accepts the Jews, who are condemned to eternal bondage due to their own fault, because they crucified the Lord, of whom the prophets had foretold that He would appear in the flesh. ... to curb the violations of the Jews so they would not dare to stick their necks out — bent beneath the yoke of eternal bondage — to confront the worthiness of belief'.*

6. 'Rag-and-bone Jews'. English caricature by Thomas Rowlandson. 18TH CENT.

7. The Jews, as serfs of the sovereign, were dependant on so-called privileges: here the Roman Jews receive privileges from Henry VII.
COUNTRIES ON THE RHINE. MINIATURE. EARLY 14TH CENT.

8. Caricature of a Jew peddling his wares from door to door.
ITALY. C. 1700.

9. German playing card lampooning a Jew, with a yellow badge and money-bag.
15TH CENT.

Chapter 6

Towards the End of the Middle Ages

Between the twelfth and the fifteenth centuries, Spain was recaptured from Islam. Throughout the country there were enforced conversions, which Jews, too, had to endure. Baptised Jews, sneeringly called *Marranos* (swine), were suspected of remaining true to Judaism in secret. The Spanish theologians devised the doctrine of *Limpieza de sangre*, the 'purity of the blood', in answer to this 'danger of heresy'. Under this doctrine, a Jew who had been baptised remained a Jew and in their eyes was a danger to society. Even great-grandchildren of *Marranos* were persecuted by the Inquisition. In 1492 Ferdinand and Isabella drove the last Spanish Jews out of their country.

The humanist Erasmus believed the Jews who were baptised were even more dangerous than those who were not: an invisible enemy in the Christian world. His greatly praised tolerance did not apply to Jews.

1. An example of the badges Jews of the late Middle Ages had to wear: a Portugese rabbi (at right, with the Torah) is wearing a red star over his breast.
PANEL BY NUNO GONCALVES. 1465.

The Valladolid Laws

In 1391, the sermons and campaigns of conversion by the Dominicans in Spain led to violence in hundreds of Jewish districts. The Dominicans then stated that these disturbances of the civil order had proved that the Jews constituted a 'problem', for which a solution had to be found. In 1412, Bishop Pablo de Santa Maria of Burgos introduced the *Laws of Valladolid* in which he decreed that the Jewish districts were to be enclosed and placed under strict control. This measure anticipated the ghettos. The Jews were also prohibited from carrying weapons and from being addressed as *Don* (sir).

They had to wear badges and men were required to let their beards grow. Jewish doctors were no longer allowed to treat Christians. There were limitations placed on business relations with Christians. The Dominican Vicente Ferrer took the Bishop's instructions to Aragon, where he was able to convince the Spanish Pope, Benedict XIII, and King Ferdinand I that it was the duty of church and state to take further measures against the Jews.

2. The expulsion decree of 1492, signed by the Spanish royal couple Ferdinand and Isabella, which banished the Jews from Spain.

3. *Auto-da-fé's* (acts of faith) took place in the Iberian peninsula into the eighteenth century. This engraving shows a public burning in Lisbon.

4. In an *auto-da-fé* heretics were burned at the stake by the Inquisition. Countless Jews were killed in Spain.
PANEL BY PEDRO BERRUGUE-TE, EARLY 16TH CENT.

5. Bearing the Cross: portrayal of Jesus as the noble victim of a primitive, dehumanized Jewish mob.
PANEL BY JEROEN BOSCH. C.1500.

Banishment of Jews from Spain

In 1478, the monarchs Ferdinand and Isabella received a papal bull from Pope Sixtus IV. He granted them permission to set up a special Inquisition in Spain, primarily intended to persecute baptised Jews who had secretly remained faithful to Judaism. For decades, the Spanish bishops had been pleading for this. Undoubtedly, many Jews who were forcibly baptised reverted to their old religious customs more or less secretly. They were suspected of heresy and regarded as enemies, and as more dangerous because they were able to camouflage themselves. The clergy felt dismayed about the behavior of the baptised Jews; they had offered Jews the possibility of escaping persecution, being burned at the stake, or banishment. The clergy had baptised them so they would be forgiven for their complicity in the murder of God, but, in their eyes, the Jews remained as stubborn and unteachable as always. The clergy were completely powerless, confronted with the Jews, whose customs and traditions flouted the sacrament of baptism. These pariahs, from whom the Church had wanted to re-

move the curse, were clearly prepared to remain faithful to the depraved belief of their fathers under the most dangerous circumstances. The Church together with the monarchs Ferdinand and Isabella, then strove for the destruction of these baptised Jews.

Thousands of *Marranos* were burned at the stake by the special Inquisition. In 1492, Ferdinand decided to banish all the Spanish Jews because Jews were accused of doing their utmost to destroy Christianity. The result of this decree was that one hundred and fifty thousand Jews were driven out of the country.

7. Later versions of *The Wandering Jew* became more and more like a caricature.
BRUSSELS. 18TH CENT.

The Legend of the Wandering Jew

The legend of the Jewish shoemaker who was cursed by God because he had ridiculed Jesus during his martyrdom and had refused to let him rest at his door, appeared in Europe in the late Middle Ages. In 1602, this legend entered world literature via the work *Kurze Beschreibung und Erzählung von einem Juden mit Namen Ahasverus*, ('Short Description and Account of a Jew called Ahasverus'), printed by Christoff Creutzer at Leiden, Holland. There were different interpretations of the theme of the eternally wandering Jew who witnessed the martyrdom of Jesus. Many aspects of the hatred for Jews were absorbed into the hundreds of variations of this legend. The legend was often used by the clergy to interpret the banishment of Jews out of almost all the countries of Europe from the standpoint of religious history. The fate of the shoemaker, Ahasverus, to wander forever became a symbol of the fate of the entire Jewish people, doomed to travel through the world until the Day of Judgement. The curse that the Jewish people bore after the murder of God's Son consisted of banishment, of being driven from one country to another without a permanent place to live.

The Wandering Jew, nicknamed Ahasverus, shown in a German engraving from 1618. The legend originated in the late Middle Ages, but appeared in world literature after 1600.

8. The Inquisition compared with the Last Judgement: the Church was only doing what awaited the Jews in hell. Below left, Pope Gregory X on the throne.

Doctrine and Practice of the *Limpieza de sangre*

In the history of the Church's struggle against the Jewish religion and its followers, we can distinguish two phases.

In the first phase, the leading thinkers of the Church believed the Jew could be cleansed of the taint of murdering God through baptism. From the second half of the fifteenth century, there were important theologians in Spain who seriously doubted whether baptism would have this effect. They believed the Jew remained responsible for his people's sins, even if he was baptised. They viewed the Jews – baptised or not – as a corrupt people, their criminal behavior corresponding to their nature, which they could not belie.

Baptised Jews had become the advisers and tax collectors of sovereigns. A few had careers in the church. In 1449, a rebellion broke out in Toledo against baptised Jews as a result of Christian frustrations and jealousy. The traditional enmity and hatred resurfaced toward the people accused of being murderers of God. With an appeal to church and secular law, the Toledo city government decided that baptised Jews could no longer hold public office. In this way, the first statute of *Limpieza de sangre* ('purity of the blood') was drawn up.

Countless cities and religious orders then adopted this statute in order to keep baptised Jews out. The archbishop of Toledo, Sileceo, decreed in 1547 that baptised Jews could not practice medicine, surgery or pharmacy, because they would always be ready to murder Christians. Popes Alexander VI, Leo X, Clement VII and Paul III also approved the statute of *purity of the blood*. In Spain, Christian society was hypnotised and obsessed by this statute for almost four hundred years, and it was not abolished until the nineteenth century. A person was judged to be of *impure* descent if his mother were even one-eighth Jewish. In the seventeenth century, the obsession reached its peak. In that period, the Spanish roads were full of officials who were ordered to obtain information from passersby. The local archives were often consulted, and village elders were questioned about individuals, because they were well informed about the most intricate family relationships. The Jewish historian, Leon Poliakov, wrote in his great work, *Histoire de l'antisemistisme* of 1968: *'We can compare the racist interpretation of history, which has obsessed a sizable portion of the world this past century, to the manner in which Jewish-Christian relations were interpreted in the racist theology of the 'Limpieza de sangre'.*

of evil. The scoundrel Pfefferkorn is more than half Jewish. If you operate on him, six hundred Jews will spring out. He should have remained completely Jewish, or had his tongue and both hands circumcised like his foreskin. He is the most terrible nemesis, he is an envoy from Satan, a devilish vermin, a disguised champion of the faith. Why do real Christians associate with this mangy Jew?'*

Desiderius Erasmus

On 24 July 1986, the commemorative year for Erasmus, Professor Heiko Oberman, a church historian at the University of Tübingen, said: *'Erasmus goes much farther in his intolerance of Jews than Luther... The historian must reach that conclusion if, at least, he takes the judgement of the baptised Jew as the standard for sixteenth century antisemitism. Erasmus believed "once a Jew, always a Jew". According to Luther, Jews and non-Jews were made each other's equals through baptism.'*

Erasmus described Pfefferkorn, the Jew who had become a Christian, in a letter to Pirckheimer as follows: *'a complete lunatic, a shameless lout, whom we do not call a half-Jew, but who proves by his deeds that he is a super Jew. The devil, the eternal enemy of the Christian religion, could not have wished for a better instrument than such an angel of Satan's, who destroys the most important and the best of our religion everywhere, namely its visible unity, under the pretence that he is defending the Christian religion. I dare to wager my head that he had no other intention in having himself baptised than to act even more evilly towards Christians and – once accepted in this society – to infect the whole world with his poison. What could he have possibly achieved, if he had remained a Jew? Only now that he has put on a Christian mask, does he behave like an authentic Jew, and does he act in accordance with his origin. He is as dumb as an ox, but a real genius in the performance*

9. Erasmus of Rotterdam: this humanist's renowned tolerance did not apply to Jews.
PORTRAIT BY HANS HOLBEIN THE YOUNGER. 1530-32.

Chapter 7

Reformation and Counter Reformation

The Reformation of 1517 led to a schism in Christianity. Luther originally thought the Jews were right in not wanting to belong to the Roman Catholic Church he so despised. But when the Jews did not convert to Protestantism, he published a violently antisemitic tract, *On the Jews and Their Lies*. He called on sovereigns to banish the Jews and burn their books and synagogues.

The Counter Reformation had to win ground lost by the Roman Catholic Church. All forms of heresy: the new, such as Protestantism, and the old, such as Judaism, were violently assailed. The Jews in Rome and other cities of the Papal State were forced to live in ghettos, they had to demonstrate their submission to each new pope, and were forced to listen to sermons aimed at conversion.

1. Title page of *Der Joedenspiegel* (The Mirror of Jews) 1507, a fierce attack on the Jewish faith written by the baptised Jew Pfefferkorn. Dominicans made grateful use of this to prove the truth of Christian belief.

The Dispute between Reuchlin and Pfefferkorn about the Burning of Jewish Literature

In 1509, Pfefferkorn, a baptised Jew, started a campaign to have the Talmud burned. The Dominicans of Cologne supported his campaign. His greatest opponent in the struggle was Johannes Reuchlin, one of the most important humanists of the time. In his apology, titled *Augenspiegel*, (Mirror of the Eye), Reuchlin wrote that Jews and Christians had to be equal before the law. He referred to Roman law: Jews and their possessions should be protected even when there were ethical objections to the person in question. He therefore regarded it as contrary to Roman law to remove and burn the Jewish texts. Moreover, he thought that Hebrew literature – the Talmud and the Cabala, for instance – could serve to support the Christian faith. One of Reuchlin's arguments was weak: *'Nobody has ever wanted to condemn the Talmud.'* From the thirteenth century on, popes had often ordered Hebrew literature consigned to flames.

Then a war of pamphlets began between those who supported and those who opposed burning Hebrew literature. The Universities of Mainz, Cologne, Erfurt, Heidelberg and Paris sided with Pfefferkorn, because they wanted to remain faithful to the traditional policy of the Church, and they reproached Pope Leo X for having broken faith with his predecessors' policy. Reuchlin gained supporters among those who wanted to put medieval superstition behind them and advocated the free practice of science. In his *Brandspiegel* ('Mirror of Fire') Pfefferkorn advised that aged Jews, who could no longer be converted, be banished to an isolated place, like mangy dogs, and that children be taken away from Jews and forcibly baptised. To this proposal of Pfefferkorn and his supporters, Reuchlin answered: *'I do not want Jews to act unjustly, but neither do I want them to suffer injustice. When people abandon legal norms, they become like wild animals'.* On 26 July 1516, the Pope and bishops present at the Lateran Council in Rome acquitted Reuchlin of heresy.

Martin Luther

There are scarcely more bitterly anti-Jewish writings to be found in all Christian literature than those of the sixteenth century reformer, Martin Luther. Because Luther was disappointed in the Jews who did not want to convert, and he had heard that many Christians (especially in Bohemia) had converted to Judaism, he wrote *On the Jews and their Lies* in 1543, at the end of his life. In this, Luther delineated the following anti-Jewish policy:

'What must we do with this cursed and vile race of Jews? They live among us and we know that they lie, slander and swear. We can not tolerate them, if we do not want to share in their lies, their curses and their slander. Moved by prayer and respectful piety, we must act with merciful severity. Let me give you my honest advice. In the first place, their synagogues should be burned down and what does not burn must be covered with mud. This must be done for the honor of God and Christianity, so that God may see that we are Christians and we have not simply tolerated or approved that His Son and His Christians have been subjected to lies, curses, and slander.'

'In the second place, their houses should be pulled down and destroyed. They must be housed in stables like gypsies, so that they realize they are not masters of our country, as they proudly say, but unfortunate prisoners, so they will complain to God continuously.'

'Third, their books should be taken from them. Fourth, rabbis should be forbidden

2. Title page of Martin Luther's *'Von den Juden und iren Lügen'* (On the Jews and Their Lies).
WOODCUT BY LUCAS CRANACH. WITTENBERG. 1543.

to give any more lessons on pain of death. Fifth, they should not be allowed to move around freely. Let them stay home. Sixth, they should no longer be allowed to charge interest. The money that is taken from them should be spent to help Jews who agree to be baptised. Seventh, they should be put to work.'

Luther ended: *'Respected sovereigns and nobles who have Jews in your domain: if this advice does not suit you, look for something better, so that you and all of us will be freed from this unbearable, devilish burden, the Jews.'*

Even though most of the sovereigns ignored the advice Luther gave, many since the Reformation have referred to his authority to legitimize their hatred toward Jews.

3. The reformer Martin Luther, a bitter antisemite when he was older.
PANEL BY LUCAS CRANACH. 16TH CENT.

The Burning of Hebrew Literature by the Popes of the Counter Reformation

Pope Julius III (1550-1555) realized that the advent of printing made it possible for Hebrew literature to be circulated on a large scale. In his opinion, this development endangered the existence of the Church. Thousands of Hebrew manuscripts were printed in Italian cities and sold in many European countries. When the Franciscan Cornelio de Montalcino became Jewish, the cardinals advised Pope Julius III to burn Hebrew literature to prevent more Christians from embracing the Jewish religion. As so often in the past, it was the conversion of Christians to the Jewish religion that was the direct motivation for taking anti-Jewish measures. Even before copies of the Talmud were confiscated, the inquisitors of the *Holy Office* (Inquisition in Rome) had had the former Franciscan monk burned at the stake.

When all the Hebrew books had been removed from synagogues and houses, this was celebrated on 9 September 1553, the Jewish New Year. Pope Julius III organized a huge *auto-da-fé* on the Campo dei Fiori at which the Hebrew literature of hundreds of Jewish writers was burned. An *auto-da-fé*, literally an 'act of faith', was the technical term the Church gave to the burning of heretics and/or their writings. A few days later, the Holy Office ordered all Catholic sovereigns, bishops and Inquisitions to confiscate and burn copies of the Talmud. This edict was not obeyed everywhere, but in the market squares of Venice, Pesaro, Urbino, Ancona, Cremona and Ferrara, thousands of books written by Jewish scholars were thrown in the fire, while the clergy sang psalms. In 1559, Paul IV ordered that all Jewish texts be burned, and Pope Pius V had twenty thousand copies of the Tal-

mud burned. The campaign of the popes against Hebrew literature continued for centuries.

Pope Paul IV and the Ghettos

The ghetto is a Jewish district, a section of a city where originally Jews lived voluntarily and to which they were later confined. Even in antiquity, separate districts for Jews existed, as in Alexandria and Rome. In Morocco the Jews were confined to the so-called *Mellahs*. In Germany at the end of the thirteenth century, special city districts were designated where Jews were forced to live, separate from Christians. This was the case in Frankfurt, Worms, Speyer, Regensburg and Nürnberg. In countless synods, bishops decreed that Jews were prohibited to live among Christians; in Breslau in the second half of the thirteenth century, they declared that the Jews in Poland had to live in walled-off districts. After April 1516, Venetian Jews were forced to settle in a separate district. The word *ghetto* is probably derived from the Italian *gietto*, as the artillery foundery was called that had been situated there.

But it was Pope Paul IV who made a prison of the Jewish district of Rome in his bull of 12 July 1555: between sunrise and sunset the gates of the walled-off district were bolted. The Jews had to pay for building the walls and both gates themselves. The ghetto lay on the bank of the Tiber and was

4. The Roman Jews humbly presented each new Pope with a copy of the Scrolls of the Law and had to request he confirm the favors he had granted them.
ETCHING BY PICART. C 1650.

5. A compulsory conversion sermon in Rome, customary for centuries.
WATERCOLOR BY HIERONYMUS HESS. 1829.

PORTICVS SINAGOGAE
IVDAICAE RATISPONEN
FRACTA 21 DIE FEB
ANN 1519

6. After an alleged desecration of a Host, the synagogue in Regensburg had to be destroyed in 1519. Altdorfer made this print just before the demolition. A Maria Chapel was then built on the spot.

Jews for the murder of God's Son. By order of the same Paul IV, in one city after the other – Florence, Mantua, Padua and Ferrara – Jews were confined to ghettos. Outside the ghetto, they were required to wear a badge for identification.

Banishment of the Jews from the Cities of the Papal State and Other Cities in Italy

Pope Pius V (1566-1572) conformed increasingly to the anti-Jewish politics of the Spanish sovereigns, Ferdinand and Isabella. He conceived of banishing all Jews from the Papal State, as Catholic sovereigns had done before him in England, France, Spain and Portugal.

But when the Pope announced these plans, the cardinals immediately voiced their criticism. They reminded him that the ghetto in Rome had to be preserved as a symbol of God's eternal anger at the Jewish people. Prominent citizens of the harbor city, Ancona, informed the Pope that the Jews living there formed the most important link in the future economic growth of the Papal State, and that their banishment would lead to bankruptcy. The Pope then ordered that the Jews be driven from the cities of the Papal State, with the exceptions of Rome and Ancona.

Pope Pius V was not the first Italian to have the Jews banished: in 1497, the Jews of Venice were summoned to leave the city; this was repeated in Genoa in 1516 and 1550, in the Kingdom of Naples in 1540, and in the duchies of Ferrara and Milan in 1597. However it was often a game of in-again, out-again. If it was primarily the clergy who promoted their banishment, it was often the merchants who promoted their return.

tiny, only about two and a half acres. Families were forced to live in one room with all the consequences that had on privacy and hygiene. Moreover, there were annual floods of the Tiber. The ghetto was permitted only one synagogue, which restricted the conditions for religious instruction.

Sam Wagenaar, in his book *The Jews of Rome* (1974) wrote: *'The ghetto was a concentration camp to a certain extent, somewhat modified by a few insignificant freedoms.'* The Jews in Rome lived under these disgraceful circumstances until 1848. According to the popes, it was necessary that they bear witness to God's continuous punishment of

7. An early portrayal of
book-burning, conducted
by the Dominicans. The
writings of Jews and
heretics were regularly
burned.
PANEL BY BERRUGUETE.
15TH CENT.

8. The plundering of the Judengasse, the Frankfurt ghetto, in 1614. Immediately afterwards the Jews were driven out of Frankfurt.

Plünderung der Iudengaſſen zu Franckfurt am Main den 22 Auguſtj 1614. Nach Mittag vmb 5 uhr von den Handtwercks geſellen angefangen, vnd die gantze Nacht durch Continuirt, da dan ein Bürger vnd 2 Iuden gar todt blieben, viel aber beiderſeits beſchedigt worden, biſz ihn entlich, als ſie bis in die helſft der gaſſen komen, von der Burgerſchafft gentzlich abge.,

Einführung der Jüden in ihre Gassen, So der Herrn Kay[f]: Commissarien Aufschu[f], mit
Pfeiffen, Trummen vnd Fliegender Fahnen, Nach verrichter Execution, beneben etlichen
Reisigen, begleitet hat, alda ihnen ihre Stetigkeit vorgelesen, vnd die Keyser[l]
Wapen ahn ihre Thor ahngeschlagen worden, 28. Feb: A: 1616.

9. In February 1616 the
Jews were allowed to re-
turn to Frankfurt. While
they reenter the Judengasse, the Emperor's coat of
arms is nailed to the en-
trance gate.

Chapter 8

The Enlightenment and the French Revolution

The eighteenth century philosophers of the Enlightenment advocated equal civil rights and freedom of religion. However the most prominent of them, with Voltaire in the forefront, regarded Judaism as incompatible with the principles of human reason and progress. The image Voltaire had of Jews was determined by centuries of antisemitism: he condemned the Jews not because they were not Christians, but because they were traditionally regarded as despicable and greedy for money.

Those who supported civil rights for Jews hoped that they would free themselves in this way of the *Jewish nature* attributed to them. Others required they give up their *Jewish mentality* as a prerequisite for their acceptance in society.

The French Revolution of 1789 gave the Jews equal civil rights. In the countries later occupied by France, the German states for example, this emancipation was regarded as an undesirable product of the occupation and was often annulled after the departure of the French.

1. 'The London Exchange Receives Bad News.' ANONYMOUS ANTISEMITIC COLOR ETCHING FROM ENGLAND. C. 1780.

2. Rules for 'The New Game of the Jew', a dice game that emerged in England in 1807.

3. The second expulsion of the Jews from Prague in 1745. The ghetto was often plundered before the Jews were first expelled in 1541.

Voltaire

In 1757, the French philosopher, Voltaire, published his *Dictionnaire philosophique* (Philosophical Dictionary). Of one hundred and eighteen articles, thirty were concerned with various facets of the Jewish religion and Jews. In one of these articles he wrote: *'The Jews are nothing more than an ignorant, barbarian people, who combine the foulest greed with a terrible superstition and an uncompromising hatred of all the peoples who tolerate them and at whose cost they even enrich themselves.'*

He judged the Jewish religion by four standards. The first standard was morality: the Jews of biblical times were guilty of atrocities (such as human sacrifice) and deceit, but also of sexual perversity. The second standard was reason: a God who required ritual acts from the Jews such as making sacrifices, observing the Sabbath, conforming to dietary laws and circumcision, and one, moreover, who imposed heavy sanctions on violations of these, was contrary to the image that enlightened thinkers formed of a God. The third standard was scientific and cultural creativity: the Jews had never, in his opinion, contributed anything to the development of science and culture. The fourth standard was politics: the mere fact that the Jewish people were sent into exile three times should make enlightened thinkers conclude that the Jews were incapable of forming their own state.

Voltaire's judgment about the development of the Jewish religion in later times was even more negative:

5. 'Jewish Greed'.
MANCHESTER, ENGLAND,
1773.

4. A new theme in antisemitic imagery is *the lecherous Jew*. 'Solomon Amusing Himself with Two Attractive Christian Girls.'
THOMAS ROWLANDSON. C. 1800.

'While the Arabs are distinguished by courage, hospitality and humanity, the Jews are cowardly and lecherous, greedy and miserly. Because the Jews managed to appropriate the wealth of all the countries by means of trade and usury, they have rightly been driven out of all the countries. The practise of usury stems from their religion. It is no wonder that wherever Jews have been admitted, people have discovered they were terrible and despised their religion.'

Isaac de Pinto, who belonged to the Portugese Jewish community in Amsterdam and who was a great admirer

of Voltaire, asked him to retract his accusations about the Jews. But Voltaire refused. De Pinto wrote him in 1762: *'Is the damage caused by the pen less harmful than the flames? Is its harm not even more consuming than the fire, because it will be relayed to future generations? What can this unhappy people expect from the mob, when barbarian prejudices are even shared by the most famous genius of our enlightened time?'*

Advocates and Opponents of Emancipation

The arguments for and against the emancipation of Jews can all be found in the discussion about the Jewish writer and philosopher, Moses Mendelssohn (1729-1786). As a boy of fourteen, Mendessohn had left for Berlin and had studied mathematics, Latin, French, German and English from rabbis. He was the first to translate the Torah from Hebrew into German. The philosophical and literary writings of Mendelssohn made him esteemed throughout Europe, especially among the supporters of the Enlightenment. But this esteem could not alter the fact that when he entered Dresden, for example, he had to pay a special entrance tax, which was just as much for a Jew as for a Polish ox, he bitterly noted. Mendelssohn advocated the acceptance of Jews in society and the abolishment of all legal regulations that stood in the way.

He received support from a friend, the Prussian archivist, Christian Wilhelm Dohm, in his book, *Die Bürgerliche Verbesserung der Juden* ('The Improvement of Jews as Citizens') in 1781. Dohm thought that if the persecution of Jews ceased, they would give up their Jewish customs and religious observances as a matter of course. If the Jews were freed of their chains, he stated, they would quickly

Der Unterricht.

Clavierlehrer. „Sie sind nicht aufmerksam, hier steht ein Achtel und Sie nehmen ein Viertel."

Vater (im Hintergrund). „Ganz meine Natur, warum soll sie nemme a Achtel, wenn sie kann hawwe a Viertel?!"

prefer the righteous state to their religion. At the same time, this expectation showed the limits of emancipation: as individuals, Jews could be emancipated by ceasing to be Jews.

Opponents of emancipation stated that Jews could never become loyal citizens because their moral perversity, the result of their stubborn adherence to the Talmud, had entered their bloodstream, and for that reason they were eternally persecuted.

Later in life Mendelssohn was chosen for membership in the Berlin Academy of Science, but Frederick the Great refused to give him the personal approval required for admittance.

6. The piano lesson. The teacher: 'You are not paying attention: this is an eight and you're taking a quarter.' Father: 'It's only her nature. Why should she take an eight if she can get a quarter?'
FROM 'FLIEGENDE BLÄTTER'. C. 1850.

7. Cartoon about emancipation. 'The Jew Stands Watch.' The Jewish soldier runs away while being relieved.
VIENNA. 1848.

Ged. b. K. Horegsery

Der Jüd af der Wocht.

geschrien Wai! zu Hilf! se machen mich dodt! Wai! jetzt is losgangen! iach riech schon s'Pülfer:
kommandant) Aber Schabs'l kenst mich den nicht iach bin ja der Herschl, mer kümmen ja ablösen.

The French Revolution and the Jews

The views of Dohm (see above) and enlightened philosophers such as Mirabeau had great influence on Abbé Grégoire. After the French Revolution of 1789, the question under discussion was whether the *Declaration of the Rights of Man and the Citizen* also pertained to Jews. In the National Assembly, Abbé Grégoire pleaded that Jews be given exactly the same rights. Conservative opponents stated that the Jews were a separate people and that in their case, the rights for aliens ought to apply. After a delay of two years, however, the Jews received their full civil rights. When in 1792 the first Jew was elected to the National Assembly, he was welcomed by the chairman's congratulations on being a free citizen, freed of all preconceptions and traditions.

Napoleon was under great pressure to repeal the rights for Jews, especially from the Alsace where several thousand East European Jewish refugees were living. On a visit to Strasbourg, he heard reports about Jewish speculators. Without any further investigation or any respect for persons, Napoleon enacted restrictive trade measures in 1808 for all Jews: the so-called *Décret Infâme* ('the Infamous Decree').

The position of Jews was also on the agenda of the Congress of Vienna, which met after the military defeat of Napoleon in 1815. It was decided that the *adherents of the Jewish religion* would eventually receive the same rights and duties, but that the rights would be limited to those granted by the separ-

8. Cartoon directed at Jews who sought acceptance in bourgeois society during the Enlightenment, taking dancing lesson, for instance: 'Dalles and His Family.' LATE 18TH CENT.

9. Anti-Jewish riots and plundering in Frankfurt. After the French withdrawal, antisemitism increased in Germany. 1819.

ate German states before they were occupied. One effect of this was that the rights granted by France were repealed.

In France itself, the *Décret Infâme* was repealed and Jews again received full civil rights. In the German states and Austria, the situation became completely confused. The legal position of Jews there varied from one of equal rights to one with restrictions that went back to the Middle Ages. In Prussia alone there were more than eighteen regulations on Jews in effect.

Chapter 9

Political Antisemitism in the Nineteenth Century

Many Jews enthusiastically took part in the struggle for civil rights in the nineteenth century and were active in Liberal Parties. Conservatives regarded Liberalism as suspect precisely because of this Jewish support. They rejected it as a *Jewish product*.

But anti-Jewish views were also not exceptional among Liberals and Socialists. The ancient equation of Judaism with moneylending sometimes led to a rejection of capitalism on the basis of antisemitic arguments. Karl Marx, son of a Jewish lawyer who became Protestant, also equated the two. Antisemitic ideas were like a thread that ran through the works of early Socialist thinkers such as Fourier and Proudhon.

Between 1848 and 1870, the Jews in Western Europe, except for Germany and Austria, received full civil rights. The ghettos were abolished, all studies and occupations were declared open to Jews: emancipation was a fact.

At the end of the nineteenth century however, antisemitic parties in Germany, France and Austria achieved unexpected success. Antisemitism became an attractive plank in party platforms. During the trial of Dreyfus, a Jewish French officer accused of treason in 1894, antisemitic views played so great a role that many Jews thought that emancipation had failed permanently.

1. A German print from the revolutionary year 1848: the Devil, the Sovereign, the Church and the Jew form a pact against progress.

Antisemitism in Early Socialism

Like several important philosophers of the Enlightenment, some founders of Socialism regarded the Jews as an obstacle to all human progress. The French Utopian Socialist, Charles Fourier (1772-1817), who was inspired by the ideology of the medieval guilds, saw the Jews as the deceitful and unscrupulous competitors of Christians craftsmen and merchants. Fourier knew that in France usury was practiced by Christians, but he believed Jewish usury was more dangerous and the emancipation of Jews would thus be ominous. In 1808 he wrote: '*Because if the Jews possess even a quarter of the capital, as a result of their secret and indissoluble bonds they will exercise the greatest influence.*' In a book which became popular, *Les Juifs, Rois de l'Epoque* ('The Jews, Kings of the Century') of 1844, Fourier's student, Toussenel, turned against the domination of money, which he equated with Jewish domination: '*I indicate with this contemptible name "Jew" every moneylender, every parasite averse to productive activity who… lives off the work of his fellow humans.*' The Christian Socialist, Pierre Leroux, published a book of the same title two years later. He wrote: '*We want to act against the Jewish spirit and our statements are certainly not directed at the Jews as a collection of individuals, or against this or that Jew in particular. The Jewish spirit, a spirit of egoism, penetrates the whole society and can only be suppressed by Socialism.*'

The tradition of French Socialists was shared by their German colleagues. Karl Marx (1818-1883) also equated Judaism with huckstering, usury and egoism, and with profiteering, alienation and capitalism. Marx envisioned a society which would make Jews impossible. In his brochure *Zur Judenfrage* (on the Jewish Question) of 1844, he called Judaism the current antisocial element. '*What*

is the profane basis of Judaism? Practical need, selfish interest. What is the worldly cult of the Jew? Huckstering. What is his worldly god? Money.' Marx stated that humanity had to free itself of Judaism's domination: '*Jewish emancipation is in the last analysis the emancipation of humanity from Judaism.*'

Michael Bakunin (1814-1876), Marx's rival and the founder of Anarchism, wrote: '*Jews constitute a danger to Socialism; they are inclined to use Communism for the establishment of state capitalism.*'

2. Election poster by Willette, 'antisemitic candidate … against Jewish tyranny.'
FRANCE. 1889.

3. Adolf Stoecker, imperial court preacher in Berlin and antisemitic leader, on his Silver Anniversary.
1893.

4. Karl Lueger, the popular burgomaster of Vienna at the turn of the century, chosen on an antisemitic platform.
WATERCOLOR BY WILHELM GAUSE. 'THE PAGEANT OF FLOWERS''. 1904.

Social-Christian Antisemitism

At the end of the nineteenth century, Adolf Stoecker, court preacher in Berlin, was active in missionary work in the city. Stoecker was deeply convinced that Germany could only fulfill its great mission as a Christian nation if the socio-economic situation of the workers changed. How did the workers and the lower middle classes land in such a miserable situation? Stoecker blamed modern Judaism. Influenced by the Jews, the working class also worshipped money. The social struggle of Stoecker and his supporters against economic exploitation thus became a struggle against the alleged Jewish domination of German society. In a speech given in 1883, he said: *'I know very well that the liberal press – the Jews and those who conspire with them – brand us as "Jew-baiters" and regard me as the leader of this group. But I count myself fortunate that here in Berlin I have made a start on halting the Jewish domination of society. The Jews are guilty because they provoke the peoples of the world to the extreme. The antisemitic movement is sweeping across the whole earth. Gentlemen, everywhere the domination by Jews has become unbearable, people rise to throw off this yoke. We declare war on the Jews to conquer them completely, and we shall not rest before they have been toppled from the high pedestal on which they have placed themselves here in Berlin into the dust where they belong.'*

Stoecker felt called upon to carry on and renew the Lutheran tradition in which he was raised. The Jewish suffering had a twofold purpose for the court preacher from Berlin: it served *'for the honor and strengthening of our faith and to shame the belief of Jews who obstinately persevere in their unbelief.'* Stoecker advocated barring all Jews from holding public office.

5. Caricature 'Jews Bring the Downfall of Frankfurt.' Well known Jews of Frankfurt are shown who had struggled for democracy and equal rights. 1853.

6. The famous 19th century illustrator, Gustave Doré, also handled the theme *The Wandering Jew*. COLORED WOODCUT. 1852.

7. The result of the French Revolution, as the antisemitic artist Caran d'Ache saw it: the farmer, first oppressed by the nobility, is now oppressed by the Jew. END 19TH CENT.

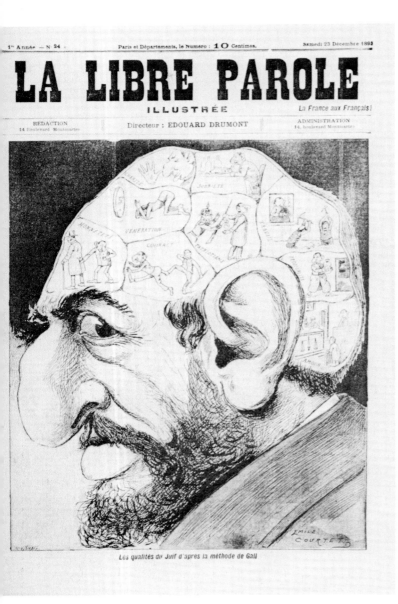

1re Année — N° 24 · Paris et Départements, le Numéro : **10** Centimes. Samedi 23 Décembre 1893

LA LIBRE PAROLE
ILLUSTRÉE
La France aux Français!

RÉDACTION
14 Boulevard Montmartre

Directeur : EDOUARD DRUMONT

ADMINISTRATION
14, boulevard Montmartre

Les qualités du Juif d'après la méthode de Gall

8. *La Libre Parole* ('The Free Word'), a widely distributed antisemitic magazine edited by Edouard Drumont, on the eve of the Dreyfus affair. 1893.

9. From the periodical *Psst...* published by Caran d'Ache. The judges in the Dreyfus case: 'Silence, gentlemen, a Frenchman is arriving...' 1899.

The Dreyfus Affair

Because Jews did not have their own country and were widely scattered, they were regularly accused of being traitors. Martin Luther, for instance, accused the Jews of treason when Europe was threatened by the Turks in the sixteenth century. In December 1894 in France, the Jewish army captain, Alfred Dreyfus, was charged with having passed military secrets to the Germans. According to the charge, the proof for this was an unsigned note a cleaning woman was said to have found in a wastebasket in the German Embassy. Although the handwriting did not at all resemble that of Dreyfus, he was arrested, charged with treason and sentenced to life imprisonment in the penal colony, Devil's Island. While a small group of Frenchmen were deeply convinced of Dreyfus' innocence, and believed that another officer, Esterhazy, was the guilty one, the majority of their countrymen believed that Dreyfus had committed high treason.

The famous writer, Emile Zola, was among those who became convinced of Dreyfus' innocence. Zola, who had a deep loathing for the politics of the French clergy and was a supporter of humanist Socialism, wrote a series of articles in the newspaper *Le Figaro* in 1896-1897 to defend the Jews. One of his statements became famous: '*Because the Jews have been persecuted by us for eighteen centuries, they are what they are today.*' His struggle against antisemitism in France reached a peak when, on 13 January 1898, he published an open letter to President Félix Faure on the front page of the radical daily *L'Aurore*. It began with the words: *J'accuse* ('I accuse...'). He went on to accuse the French government and the army of having violated the truth. He said they should really be put on trial for high treason for having betrayed humanity.

In June 1899, the case was reopened, forgery was proved and Dreyfus' punishment was reduced to ten years. Dreyfus, however, was not rehabilitated until 1906. Theodor Herzl wrote in his journal: *'The Dreyfus affair illustrates not only an aberration of justice, it also illustrates the desire of the majority of the French to persecute one Jew, and through him, all Jews. Death to the Jews, cried the mob when the stripes were torn from his captain's uniform... when a progressive and doubtlessly highly cultivated people can come to this, what can be expected of other peoples?'* The big outburst of antisemitism did not come until after the publication of the letter from Emile Zola. Jewish shops were plundered and Jews were assaulted.

Chapter 10

The Racial Doctrine and the Myth about the Jewish Conspiracy

The so-called racial theories came into existence from about the middle of the nineteenth century. A variety of quasi-scientific works claimed that the struggle between the races was the key to world history. People were said to be good or bad because of the race they belonged to, not arbitrarily. Some works even claimed that only the pure *Aryan* race (Caucasian or Germanic) was the supreme conveyer of culture. Jewry was interpreted as being a separate race, called *Semitic*, and its goal, even that of those who had converted, was to undermine and destroy Aryan culture. In this manner, Jews were no longer condemned on religious grounds, but on so-called scientific grounds.

In 1853, the French writer de Gobineau published *Essay on the Inequality of the Human Races*. This was particularly influential.

At the end of the nineteenth century, the *Protocols of the Elders of Zion*, an imaginary account of a secret meeting of rabbis, appeared in Russia. It was made to appear as if Jews had plotted to dominate the world. The *Protocols* combined ancient Christian anti-Jewish prejudice with the new antisemitic attitudes of racial doctrine.

1. Victims of a pogrom in the Ukraine, Russian Empire.
1905.

Racist Antisemitism and Paul de Lagarde

According to Aryan theory, the vague concept 'Aryan' was said to refer to an original tribe in the Himalayas, which was the cradle of the Caucasian race. The French writer, Ernest Renan, stated that the 'Semitic' mind was superficial, while that of the 'Aryan' was rational and wise. By the middle of the nineteenth century, the attitude that there was a dichotomy between 'Aryans' and 'Semites' had become commonplace. In the thinking of racist antisemites, the 'Aryan' and the 'Jew' were as far apart as humans and animals. When they wrote about Jews, they discussed mice, rats, lice, beasts of prey, grasshoppers, spiders, bloodsuckers – in short, vermin; but also abcesses, plague bacilli, virus, TB, syphilis and cancer. In contrast to the noble 'Aryan', the Jew was no longer a human being, but a symptom of decay. What various influential thinkers had reproached Jews for in past centuries (see, for example, the sections about Chrysostom and Martin Luther) was no longer blamed on their religion but on their *'Jewish blood'*.

The orientalist Paul de Lagarde (1827-1891), became the prophet of a new German religion. In his publication of 1878, *Die Religion der Zukunft* ('The Religion of the Future'), he developed his ideas. According to him, Christianity had become Judaized, and because of this it failed seriously in all aspects of life, spiritual as well as moral. He wrote: *'Every Jew is proof of the weakness of our national life and of the limited value of what we call the Christian religion.'* In the program of the Conservative Party in Prussia in 1884, he urged '... *the destruction of Jewry...*' because otherwise Europe would become one huge graveyard. He summoned his contemporaries to wreck the synagogues. In his *Die nächsten Aufgaben der deutschen Politik* ('The Next Task for German Politics'), he advocated the deportation of all Jews to Madagascar. He thought it was senseless to argue with Jews. He wrote: *'Because Jews are bacilli and tapeworms, they should be eliminated as soon as possible.'* Hitler and his ideologist, Rosenberg, were great admirers of de Lagarde.

2. The composer Richard Wagner, champion of a *Germanic* art, and author of *Das Judenthum in der Musik* (Jewry in Music) under the pseudonym K. Freigedank (1850).
BUST BY ARNO BREKER.

Wagner and Antisemitism

The composer Richard Wagner, who was inspired by his friend Bakunin, with whom he participated in the civil revolution of 1848 in Dresden, dreamed of a more radical revolution through art. In 1850, Wagner published the brochure, *Das Judentum in der Musik* ('Jewry in Music'), in which he attacked the Jewish influence on German culture in general, and on music in particular. In this work and in his later ideological and cultural essays about what he intended in writing his operas, he unfolded his view of the world. Wagner, among whose friends

3. Pamphlet in which Richard Wagner, throwing himself into the breach for *Germanic* art, is attacked by three horseflies representing the Jewish composers Meyerbeer, Mendelssohn and Offenbach.
LEIPZIG. 1869.

were a few Jews, wrote in defense of '... *that instinctive dislike...*', '... *the involuntary repellance the nature and personality of the Jews possess for us.*' He described the Jews as '... *former cannibals, now trained to be the business agents of society.*'. As *eternal aliens* they corrupted the language of the country where they had lived for generations. Their nature made them incapable of penetrating to the essence of things. Because they missed the capacity for true creation, they could only imitate.

In his view of the world, Wagner assigned Jews a unique and completely despicable role. He rejected their ethical code because it gave man feelings of guilt about healthy powers and instincts. With its concept of conscience, Judaism had saddled the world with a slave mentality and an obnoxious sympathy for the weak. Law and morality robbed man of his freedom and of authentic love. He wrote: '*Grecian freedom, strength and beauty...*' had been destroyed, men had become enslaved: '... *thus we are slaves until this very day.*' Europe, once completely pagan and therefore completely free, had been enslaved by the Jewish God through Christianization.

By means of his operas, Wagner wanted to achieve the liberation of the unconscious natural instincts and to create a new world, free from the burden of Jewish ethics, in which the strong individual would be his own god, and his instincts would be his only law. Lacking box office success at first, Wagner gave a Christian varnish to his operas with their pagan gods and goddesses.

Various characters in his operas, such as Mime and Alberich in the *Ring der Nibelungen*, and Kundry and Klingsor in *Parsival* were antisemitic caricatures, as Wagner's detailed stage directions showed. Mime was presented in the libretto as a Jewish character: '*Do I stammer or stumble over my words? I take the utmost trouble hypo-*

critically to hide my innermost thoughts... Before my nodding head the world will bow, before my anger it will tremble away.' Mime's name and speech defect pointed to Wagner's idea that Jews were only able to imitate and that they corrupted the language. Alberich, who could not experience love, only lust (just like his brother), dreamed of power, too: '*When I storm the heights of Valhalla with Hella's army, I shall rule the world.*' Both perish miserably.

5. Title page of a German magazine *Ostara*. c. 1900. Caricature of the Jew and the Teuton, with the question: 'Germans! Who must lead, who must be duke?' *Ostara* called itself the 'Library for Blondes'; Adolf Hitler was a faithful reader.

6. Racial theorists devided people into higher and lower races who supposedly even had different bottoms.

Developments in Russia under the Czars

The Russian Orthodox Church played an important role in maintaining extremely anti-Jewish attitudes in Russia for centuries. The Church identified itself entirely with *Holy Russia*, and because even the presence of Jews would debase this *Holy Russia*, they were not allowed to settle there.

Through the partition of Poland at the end of the eighteenth century, Russia gained large territories where hundreds of thousands of Jews lived who were not allowed to leave the area they settled. The Jews in this limited territory were reduced to poverty through overpopulation and especially high taxes. In the first half of the nineteenth century, the authorities tried to assimilate the Jews into Russian society by converting them. Through granting extra privileges to baptised Jews, enforced conversions, and compulsory military service (for a period of twenty-five years) for which thousands of Jews were kidnapped, Czar Nicholas I hoped that the Jews would give up their Judaism. From that time Jews were also allowed to attend the Christian state-schools. When even these measures led to the baptism of only a few Jews, the idea of the incurably obstinate Jew again spread.

The abolishment of serfdom under Czar Alexander II in 1861 resulted in great social and economic changes. Agriculture changed from a feudal society to a monetary economy. The farmers were free, but before long, they suffered from the burden of heavy taxes and debts. Many of the destitute moved to the cities. The authorities tried to shift the responsibility for all the social and economic difficulties to the Jews, especially after the murder of Alexander II in 1881 by revolutionaries. The rights the Jew had gained, step by step, were repealed. In the 1880s, countless pogroms took place in the Ukraine. In 1891, all Jews were expelled from Moscow.

After the defeat of Russia by Japan in 1905, regarded as inconceivable, the violence of anti-Jewish atrocities increased.

The Myth of the Jewish Conspiracy

The myth about a Jewish conspiracy to enslave all Christians or to exterminate them originated during the Middle Ages. Jews were said to have poisoned wells to eradicate Christians. Various stories circulated in which the specter of such a conspiracy was evoked. From the Renaissance on, this myth was used for political purposes primarily in Spain, and after the French Revolution, in France and Germany, too. In 1639, Francisco de Quevedo wrote *La Isla de los Monopantos* ('The Island of the Monopantos'), in which the Jews were portrayed as dangerous conspirators. When, in 1807, Napoleon convened the *Great Sanhedrin* (a council of rabbis and Jewish scholars), opponents of the revolution accused the Jews of wanting to overthrow the traditional Christian establishment. In the second half of the nineteenth century, reactionary French Catholics, among them Barruel and Baily, wrote that Jews and Freemasons had conspired to exterminate Christians. Barruel wrote his *Mémoire pour servir à l'histoire du jacobinisme* ('Memoirs to Serve the History of Jacobinism'), to warn the Catholics in his country about this conspiracy. In Germany from 1868,

7. French edition of the *Protocols of the Elders of Zion*: 'The Jewish Danger.' 1934.

the *Rede der Grossrabbiner auf dem Judenfriedhof zu Prag* ('Speech by the Chief Rabbi in the Jewish Cemetery in Prague') by the novelist Herman Goedsche was widely circulated. In this imaginary speech, the Chief Rabbi was said to summon all the Jews in the world to strive for world domination by means of war and revolution. In the last decade of the nineteenth century, an unknown writer who worked for the *Ochrana* (the Russian secret police) in Paris wrote the *Protocols of the Elders of Zion* to influence the policies of Czar Nicholas II in regard to Jews. The writer plagarized the French journalist Maurice Joly's book from 1864, *Dialogue aux enfers entre Machiavel et Montesquieu, ou la politique au XIXe siècle* ('Dialogue between Machiavelli and Montesquieu in Hell, or the Politics of the 19th Century'), in which, though, not a single reference to Judaism and the Jews could be found. Joly wrote his political pamphlet against Napoleon III, whom he regarded as someone who wanted to subjugate the whole world. The writer falsified the imaginary *Dialogue* between Machiavelli and Montesquieu as *Protocols* (minutes) of a conference where rabbis plotted the route to Jewish domination of the world. When Czar Nicholas II received the text from Paris in 1905, he was deeply impressed. He did not doubt that it was genuine and wrote in the margin: *'The guiding and destructive hand of Judaism can be observed here.'* When closer examination conclusively proved it was forged, he forbade its further circulation with the argument: *'A case which is pure cannot be defended by impure methods.'* Yet in that same year of revolution, 1905, the *Protocols* were included as an appendix to the second edition of *The Advance of the Antichrist and the Kingdom of the Devil on Earth* by the Russian priest Sergij Nilus. Nilus wrote his work to attack the Russian Jews. During the Russian Revolution in 1917, the *Protocols* were widely distributed to incite the people against the 'Jewish revolution'. The pogroms that took place between 1918 and 1920 in southern Russia were justified by reference to the *Protocols*.

The *Protocols* were translated into many languages despite the fact that in 1921 an English journalist, Philip Graves, had specified that the unknown Russian writer had taken all his material from Maurice Joly's book and had conclusively proved that the *Protocols* were plagarized. No other antisemitic work was as widely circulated as the *Protocols*. In the United States, the influential and popular car manufacturer Henry Ford I had the work translated and published in 1927. Hitler and his followers used the *Protocols*, among other texts, to justify their persecution of Jews. Julius Streicher continued to publish series of fragments from the *Protocols*

Wzór okładki do broszury „W szponach komunizmu".

Po Rosji i Hiszpanji — kolej na Polskę! Trzeba ją pać we krwi! Zostawić po niej ruiny i zgliszcza! Żyd wiedzie kostuchę na żniwo do Polski! Baczmy na ten pochód i czuwajmy, bo gorze nam! Gorze!!!...

8. Illustration from the Polish edition of the *Protocols of the Elders of Zion*. 1937.

9. Rothschild as symbol of the 'Jewish desire for world domination.'.
FRENCH CARICATURE. 1898.

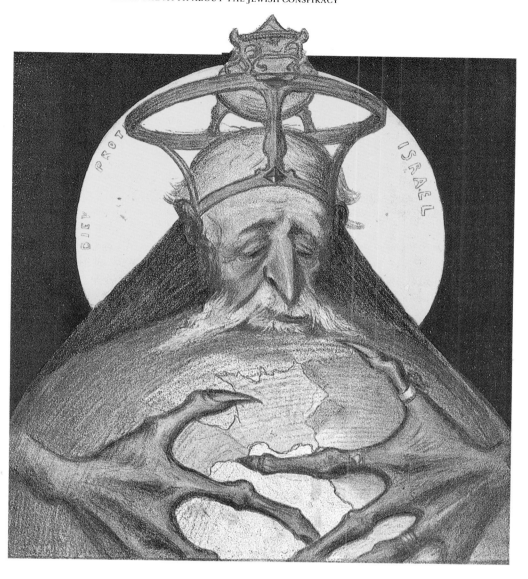

until the last days of the Third Reich. After the Second World War, the text was translated into Arabic and distributed throughout the Arab countries. In 1963, a new Spanish edition of the *Protocols* appeared which was anonymously sent to the bishops of the Second Vatican Council to prevent the Catholic Church from changing its anti-Jewish policy.

10. 'The Invisible World Government, or the Jewish Plan to Subject the World.' Spanish edition of the *Protocols*.
1930.

Nazi Antisemitism

During the years that Adolf Hitler tried to become an artist in Vienna, Karl Lueger was the popular burgomaster there. According to Hitler's book, *Mein Kampf* ('My Struggle'), published later, he became a *fanatic antisemite* in Vienna. Losing the First World War was a great blow for Germany. The National-Sozialistische Deutsche Arbeiter Partei (NSDAP), with Hitler as its leader, was one of the many parties bent on revenge. Hitler's political creed *Mein Kampf* attributed the guilt for the German defeat to the Jews. He was not alone in doing so. In the antisemitism of the NSDAP practically all the anti-Jewish stereotypes of previous centuries could be found: the Jew as usurer-capitalist, or, just the reverse, as a Socialist, as a conspirator, as a poisoner of wells. Even the Medieval myth of the ritual murder was dredged up again.

In 1933, as the majority party, the Nazis came to power. Almost all the anti-Jewish measures that were enforced had originated in past centuries: the separation of Jews from non-Jews, the exclusion of Jews from professions and studies, the special taxes, the burning of books and the wearing of badges. In 1935, the so-called Nürnberg Laws were proclaimed which prohibited all sexual relations between Jews and non-Jews.

1. An election poster for the antisemitic German party, the Völkischer Block, from 1928 shows a Jew pulling the 'strings'.

„Der Gott des Juden ist das Geld. Und um Geld zu verdienen, begeht er die größten
Verbrechen. Er ruht nicht eher, bis er auf einem großen Geldsack sitzen kann, bis er
zum König des Geldes geworden ist."

2. Interior and advertisement for the Kölner Hof Hotel in Frankfurt, Germany, c. 1905. 'Jewish patrons not welcome'.

3. The Jew as a speculator sitting on his money. From *Der Giftpilz*. 1938.

4. 'The Jewish children and teacher are expelled from school.' From a children's book, published by *Der Stürmer*. 1938.

5. Children are taught to recognize the *Jewish* nose. From the children's book *Der Giftpilz*. 1938.

„Die Judennaſe iſt an ihrer Spitze gebogen. Sie ſieht aus wie ein Sechſer..."

The Roots of Hitler's Antisemitism

Hitler's hatred of Jews was of course influenced by the great quantity of antisemitic literature he had devoured from his youth on, and which was widely available, especially in Austria. In a letter of 1919, Hitler made a distinction between emotional antisemitism and rational antisemitism. Emotional antisemitism, in his opinion, that was aroused by the sight of Jews, only ended in pogroms which yielded no result. Rational antisemitism, however, was based on hard facts and functioned very effectively. One of the hard facts was that Jews were an alien race. They lived among the Germans but they could not give up their specific characteristics. Everything Jews thought, felt and desired focussed on the material, and they used religion, Democracy and Socialism for the sole purpose of amassing money and satisfying their lust for power. Hitler was therefore enthusiastic about the *Protocols of the Elders of Zion*, regardless of whether it was authentic or forged. Rational antisemitism had to take action against the Jews' materialism and their lust for power by formulating laws to revoke the privileges which they unjustly enjoyed. Because they caused an infectious and incurable illness of the races – Hitler spoke here of *Rassentuberkulose der Völker* – through their materialism and greed for power, rational antisemitism had to focus on the total elimination of the Jews. Rational antisemitism meant putting racial antisemitism into practice.

In *Mein Kampf* (1924), nearly every page contained the idea that Jews were the cause of evil in the world, of the Treaty of Versailles and venereal diseases, capitalism and Bolshevism, social injustice and the awful cultural decay. Concerning the latter, he wrote: *'Was there really anything foul or shameless anywhere, especially in the area of culture, on which at least one Jew had not cooperated? And when such a tumor was carefully cut open, a little Jew was found like a maggot in rotting wood, who often blinked with eyes blinded by the sudden light. When I learned about the influence of Judaism on the area of art, literature, film and the theatre, I understood how great the Jewish responsibility was for their present state... because what was used here to destroy all human values was a pestilence with more fatal results than those the Black Death had had. Now the Jews serve as carriers of bacilli of the worst kind, and they infect souls everywhere. As is typical of all parasites, the Jew keeps enlarging his territory: he lives at the cost of his host and spreads like a dangerous bacillus.'*

Hitler's antisemitism was also influenced by Luther's anti-Jewish works. In March 1924, the Hoheneichen-Verlag (a publishing house) in Munich issued an unfinished manu-

6. Adolf Hitler speaks in the Bürgerbraukeller, Munich, 1925: 'The future of Germany and Our Movement'. Noted emphatically: 'No admittance for Jews.'

7. Cartoon from *Der Stürmer*. c. 1930. 'Deadly Gas above Germany,' the Nazi variation of the old accusation of poisoning.

script by Hitler's close friend, Dietrich Eckart. From this manuscript, *Gespräche mit Hitler* ('Discussions with Hilter'), it was clear that Hitler was well informed about the development of the Church's anti-Jewish doctrine and practices of the Churches during previous centuries. Eckart remarked at a certain moment that he was afraid that in reading Luther's book, *Jesus Christ Was Born a Jew*, Jews would conceive of Luther as the friend of Jewry. Hitler answered: *'I know. That is exactly the horrible tragedy. Perhaps Luther wrote his first text about the Jews in perfect innocence but he was not aware that it was precisely this book that horribly poisoned the whole European culture through the Judaization of this civilization.'* By the time Luther wrote his book, *On the Jews and Their Lies*, according to Hitler, he had seen his mistake. By then, however, it was too late, because fundamental decisions

8. Cartoon from *Der Stürmer*. c. 1930. 'The Jewish Boss in His Private Office.'

9. Front page of the 'Ritual Murder' issue of *Der Stürmer*. May 1934. All the old accusations of ritual murder are dredged up in this issue.

had been made and it was no longer possible to keep Europe *Judenrein* (free of Jews). Only at the end of his life did Luther suddenly see the Jews as people in the twentieth century saw them: in all their nakedness, as a warning for everyone and for all time. Had Luther perceived this earlier, then, at the beginning of his life, the Jews would have disappeared from the palaces of sovereigns, from the fortresses of the knights, and finally from the houses of the citizens. Eckart pointed out to Hitler in conclusion that Luther advised governments to burn down synagogues and Jewish schools. But Hitler saw no reason for that. Even if there were no more synagogues or Jewish schools, *'... the Jewish spirit would still exist and be influential. There is not a Jew, not a single Jew, who does not embody this spirit. The so-called enlightened Jews display this spirit most clearly.'* If it was really so that every Jew in Europe embodied the evil Satanic spirit, then it was not enough to set fire to synagogues and Jewish schools: each Jew had to be exterminated, as he wrote in *Mein Kampf*.

Hitler also experienced the influence of the anti-Jewish doctrine and practices of the Catholic Church. Hans Frank, one of Hitler's friends, wrote that on a lovely summer evening in 1938, Hitler said to him: *'In the Gospels, the Jews cried out to Pilate, when he refused to have Jesus crucified: "His blood be on us and on our children". Maybe I have to fulfill this curse.'* Hitler later referred to this notorious text again, saying: *'The Jews crucified Jesus, therefore it is not worthy that they should live.'* In the midst of the war, in 1942, Hitler gave a special stipend to the passion plays of Oberammergau, which were known all over Europe for their antisemitic portrayal of Judas Iscariot and the other Jews. In a letter to the director, Hitler wrote: *'The Jewish danger has seldom been more clearly illustrated than in the role of Pontius Pilate. A superior Roman, he stands there, a rock qua race and intellect amid the scum from Asia-Minor.'*

On 26 April 1933, when two bishops representing the German diocese visited Hitler, he said: *'I am being attacked for the way I treat the Jews. The Church has regarded the Jews as parasites for fifteen hundred years and has banished them to the ghetto. They knew what the Jews were worth. I am only continuing what has been happening the last fifteen hundred years. I may be doing Christianity the greatest of favors.'* And he said to Pastor Berning in 1933: *'Well, what do you really object to, in my treatment of the Jews? I have certainly been consistent. I am doing what the Catholic Church has already done for fifteen centuries. The difference between the Church and me is that I am finishing the job.'*

10. Graffiti on Jewish store during the boycott: 'Jew, Talmud-Scoundrel.'
FRANKFURT. APRIL 1933.

12. The Jew against the devil: 'Nebbish, you don't molest your own family, do you?'
DER STÜRMER. 1935.

11. 'Singer, the Jew, rapes thirty German children in Vienna.' Front page of *Der Stürmer*.
FEBRUARY 1933.

13. Book burning on the Opernplatz in Berlin.
MAY 1933.

The Antisemitic Propaganda of *Der Stürmer*

The Nürnberg paper, *Der Stürmer*, was one of the important instruments of propaganda of the NSDAP. The editor-in-chief, Julius Streicher, began his political career as editor of the paper of the Deutsche Sozialistische Partei (German Socialist Party), which offered a mixture of Socialism and antisemitism. Above all *Der Stürmer* opposed 'World Judaism' and its creation, parliamentary democracy. The paper represented Nazi antisemitism at its most extreme. In the Twenties, *Der Stürmer*, with its scandal-sheet editorial formula, achieved a circulation of twenty thousand copies, and it was the most successful of the Bavarian NSDAP-periodicals. After 1933, the paper reached a public in the millions.

Streicher and his staff drew from rich historical sources of antisemitism, especially for their illustrations. The cartoons were chosen to inspire readers with disgust for the Jews and to fix a terrifying and inhuman image of Jews firmly in their minds. The editors assured the readers time after time that the purpose of the paper was to divide the Germans from the Jews. A series of cartoons from the period between 1923 and 1933 represented themes which foreshadowed the extermination of the Jews.

14. Throughout Germany after 1933 *Der Stürmer* was publicly displayed with the slogan: 'The racial problem is the key to world history.'
DER STÜRMER.

15. Public humiliation in Hamburg on charges of so-called *Racial Defilement*, laid down in the Nürnberg Laws of 1935. On the girl's board: 'I am the filthiest woman here, I let only Jews call me dear.'

16. 'Jews not welcome! The store opposite belongs to the Jew David Boas!'

Church Leaders and Theologians and Nazi Policy

Rabbi Weismandel wrote in his memoirs about his experiences together with Rabbi Nietra in Czechoslovakia during the Second World War.

In 1942, Rabbi Nietra went to Archbishop Kametko with the request that he help prevent the Jews from being deported. The rabbi called his attention to the dangers of hunger and illness that women, the elderly, and innocent children would have to endure. Rabbi Nietra had not yet heard of gas chambers. The archbishop answered: 'It is not a question of deportation. There you will not die of hunger and misery. They will murder all of you, old and young, women and children at once – it is the punishment you deserve because you murdered our Lord and Savior, Jesus Christ. There is just one possibility of escaping this fate: convert to our religion and then I shall do my best to have the order revoked.' In 1944, Weismandel and his whole family were deported to a transit camp and from there to

Auschwitz. When he succeeded in escaping, Weismandel immediately returned to the papal nuncio to report the terrible circumstances in which thousands of children had to live in the concentration camp. The papal nuncio wanted to get rid of him and said: 'It is Sunday, a holy day for us. Tisso (the head of the government) and I do not concern ourselves with mundane affairs on such holy days.' Dazed, Weismandel wondered how the blood of innocent children could be dismissed as 'mundane'; the papal nuncio said: 'There is no innocent blood of Jewish children in the world. All Jewish blood is guilty. You have to die. This is the punishment that awaits you because of your sin.'

Professors from various disciplines and universities in Germany and Austria supported Hitler's policy in regard to the Jews. Among them were renowned theologians such as the authority on the New Testament, Gerhard Kittel. He wrote in *Die Judenfrage* (The Jewish Question) of 1933 that the history of Jewish suffering was not a lapse of European history but had its roots in the theology of Paul. He reached the conclusion, from the anti-Jewish interpretation of certain passages of the New Testament, that it was God himself who made the Jewish people suffer, because they had rejected Jesus Christ and had had him killed. Moreover, in his opinion, real followers of Christ should not resist those who were called to carry out the curse on the Jewish people under the political circumstances of 1933. He also wrote that the New Testament was *the most anti-Jewish book in the history of the world.* He interpreted the emancipation and assimilation of the Jews as expressing disobedience to God's will, because it brought an end to the banishment of the Jews, which was supposed to last until the end of the world. In 1933, he felt called upon to remind the state

17. The float with the motto 'Enemies of the People' in the carnaval parade. The Jew has been hanged.
NURNBERG. 1938.

of its solemn duty as God's instrument to restore the banishment of the Jews by law, even if the law had to be enacted in *'strenger Sachlichkeit'* (in a stricter, more businesslike way).

On 17 December 1941, the leaders of the Evangelical Church made the following declaration: *'The regulations of the "Reichspolizei" have justly branded the Jews as the born enemies of the people and of the Third Reich. From bitter experience centuries ago, Martin Luther advised governments to take strict measures against Jews and to banish them from German society. The Jews have opposed, mis-used or tampered with Christianity from the Crucifixion to the present day for their own profit. Christian baptism brings no change in the nature of a Jew, which is determined by race. Because the Evangelical Church in Germany has been ordered to give pastoral guidance to members in their religious life, it demands that Christians of the Jewish race be removed from the Evangelical Church.'* This declaration was signed by the bishop of the national churches of Sachsen, Mecklenburg, Schleswig-Holstein, Anhalt, Thüringen, and by the head of the Lutheran Church of Lübeck.

Fränkische Tageszeitung

Nürnberg · Nationalsozialistische Tageszeitung für den Gau Franken · Nr. 186 Donnerstag, 11. Aug. 1938

Julius Streicher gab das Zeichen zum Beginn des Abbruchs der Nürnberger Hauptsynagoge

Eine geschichtliche Stunde!

Die Schande von Nürnberg wird für alle Zeiten aus dem mittelalterlichen Stadtbild getilgt

Nürnberg, 10. August.

In den gestrigen Vormittagsstunden wurde der Abbruch der Nürnberger Synagoge auf dem Hans-Sachs-Platz im Rahmen einer Kundgebung des nationalsozialistischen Nürnberg begonnen. Im Mittelpunkt der Veranstaltung stand eine grundlegende und richtungweisende Ansprache Julius Streichers. Die begonnenen Arbeiten werden bis zum Beginn des kommenden Reichsparteitages bereits vollendet sein. Das Recht zu dieser notwendigen Säuberung des ehrwürdigen Nürnberger Altstadtbildes gab das Gesetz, das Nürnberg in die Reihe der deutschen Städte einordnet, deren Ausbau und Wiederherstellung im Namen des Reiches geschieht.

Wer gestern in den Vormittagsstunden durch die Stadt ging, dem fiel auf, daß das Bild des einander entgegenkommenden Verkehrs verschwunden war. Menschen, Kraftfahrzeuge und Radfahrer bewegten sich alle in einer Richtung. Sie eilten aus allen Stadtteilen einem Ziel zu: dem Hans-Sachs-Platz. Und für alle beschleunigten ihr Tempo, ja noch einen besonders guten Platz zu sichern. Tausende und aber tausende waren gekommen. Wer irgendwie seine Arbeit auf einige Stunden unterbrechen konnte, der tat es. Denn diese Kundgebung, die Rede Julius Streichers und den Beginn des Abbruchs der Synagoge wollte jeder miterleben. So war der Platz und die auflaufenden Straßen von Menschen überfüllt, die an den Sagen eines geschichtlichen Augenblickes waren.

500 Jahre zuvor, als in Nürnberg schon einmal eine Synagoge dem Erdboden gleichgemacht wurde, an deren Stelle dann die Frauenkirche entstand, war es sicher nicht anders.

Erwartung lag über allen Gesichtern. Und als zur angesetzten Zeit Julius Streicher von der Insel Schütt her auf dem Kundgebungsplatz eintraf und die Musik zu seinem Marsch anstimmte, da löste sich die Spannung in einem einzigen Aufbrausen der Heil-Rufe.

Julius Streicher dankte mit erhobener Hand für den Empfang und man sah ihm, der einst als Einsamer und Verlachter den Kampf gegen den allmächtigen Juden aufgenommen hatte, an, was ihm diese Stunde bedeutet.

Nun betrat er mit seinen Begleitern eine Empore, die vor der Synagoge errichtet worden war. Gleich darauf stand Oberbürgermeister Liebel vor dem Mikrophon und eröffnete die Kundgebung mit einer Ansprache, der wir das folgende entnehmen:

Oberbürgermeister Liebel spricht

Mein Gauleiter!

Volksgenossen und Volksgenossinnen!

Als der Gauleiter von Franken, unser frankenführer Julius Streicher, mich nach den Jahren des Kampfes im Nürnberger Rathaus mit der Führung dieser Stadt betraute...

ganzen Nürnberger Einwohnerschaft das Versprechen, daß wir alles tun würden, aus dieser Stadt wieder eine wahrhaft deutsche

Fortsetzung Seite 2

Symbolische Tat

In Nürnberg wird die Synagoge abgebrochen! Julius Streicher selbst gab durch eine mehr als einundhalbstündige Rede den Beginn der Arbeiten ein. Auf seinen Befehl löste sich dann, gewissermaßen als Auftakt des Abbruchs, der riesige Davidstern von der Kuppel. — Diese Nachrichten werden durch Draht und Funk über den Erdball jagen und werden als eine erregte Debatte, wohl als einen von innerer Anteilnahme geschriebenen Zeitungsartikel auslösen. Neben Stimmen des Jubels werden die ohnmächtigen Heulgesänge des Weltjudentums ertönen. Wieder einmal wird die ganze unsäuige Gemeinheit jüdischer Lüge und Demagogie auf Nürnberg und Julius Streicher konzentriert sein; zwei Namen, denen heute in der Welt niemand mehr achtlos vorübergehen kann.

Über Ablehnung und Zustimmung steht jedoch unverrückbar fest das Geschehen, jene symbolische Tat in den Vormittagsstunden des 10. August 1938 in Nürnberg. Was bedeutet uns der feierliche Beginn des Abbruchs der Hauptsynagoge durch Julius Streicher? Kurz gesagt: Eine historische Stunde im Kampf gegen das jüdische Weltpest? Wer glaubt, daß hier von Julius Streicher und seinen Kampfgefährten ein...

18. The *Fränkische Tageszeitung*. 11 August 1938. Julius Streicher, editor-in-chief of *Der Stürmer* announces the demolition of the largest synagogue in Nürnberg: 'An Historical Moment!'

19. A few weeks later, even before the *Week of the Broken Glass* which began with the *Kristallnacht*, the synagogue was razed.

Preparations for the 'Endlösung'

During the night of 9 to 10 November 1938, the escalation of anti-Jewish terror that had been planned took place.

Throughout Germany more than a hundred synagogues were set on fire, Jewish houses and shops were plundered, and more than 30,000 Jews were deported to camps. Fleeing the country was almost impossible shortly afterwards. As Germany attacked and occupied other European countries, one anti-Jewish measure followed the other in them, too. Clothing regulations from the Middle Ages were reintroduced: Jews were required to wear a yellow star. Internment in ghettos and ex-

pulsion and deportations had occurred earlier in European history. But the nazis went a step further. Their aim was the systematic destruction of all Jews. In Poland and the occupied territory of the Soviet Union, special execution squads, called 'Einsatzgruppen', slaughtered one Jewish community after the other in mass executions. However, that was not fast enough for the Nazis. On 20 January 1942, a meeting of top Nazis took place in the villa Wannsee in Berlin. It was resolved that European Jewry would be destroyed under the pretext of the 'Endlösung der Judenfrage', ('The Final Solution of the Jewish Problem'). All over Europe, the Jews were driven together into ghettos, robbed of everything, then deported to extermination camps and murdered in what were almost factories of death.

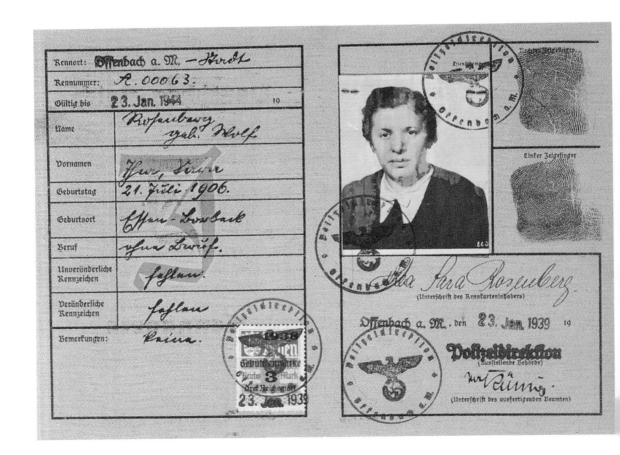

2. The synagogue of Baden-Baden during the *Week of the Broken Glass*, which began with the *Kristallnacht*. The SS rounded up and forced Jews to remove their head coverings, sing Nazi songs, and to chant in unison: 'We are a filthy, foul folk.'

The Nürnberg Laws

In 1935, the so-called Nürnberg Laws were proclaimed. The first law served: *'for the protection of German blood and honor': 'Deeply conscious that the purity of German blood is the necessary condition for the continued existence of the German people and inspired by an inflexible will to assure the existence of the German nations for all times, the Reichstag* (German Parliament) *has unanimously adopted the following law, which is hereby promulgated.*

1. Marriage between Jews and subjects of German or cognate blood is forbidden.

2. Extramarital relations between Jews and subjects of German or cognate blood are forbidden.

3. Jews may not employ in their houses women of German or cognate blood under forty-five years of age.

4. Jews are forbidden to fly the German national colors. They may, however, fly the Jewish colors: the exercise of this right is protected by the State.

5. Infractions of (1) are punishable by solitary confinement at hard labor. Infractions of (2) will be punished by imprisonment or solitary confinement at hard labor.'

A week later, regulations followed applying to *'citizens of mixed blood'*.

Although the Nazis had various theories about *Jewish blood* and *the Jewish race*, there is no such thing as a Jewish race. That was apparent from the criteria the Nazis used to determine who was Jewish: 'Jewish blood' (supposedly a biological criterion) was determined on the basis of whether the grandparents were or had been registered in a Jewish religious community, which was an administrative criterion.

In figuring out who was a Jew or of *mixed blood*, the National Socialists often appealed to church archives. Churches cooperated loyally in sorting out those with pure, less pure and impure 'blood'. The complaints from the churches concerned the amount of work involved: these complaints were accompanied by requests for remuneration. The sorting and registration which were based on the

1. The identity card for Jews, stamped with a red 'J'. Introduced in summer 1938.

3. The burning of the great synagogue of Frankfurt on the Börneplatz.
9 NOVEMBER 1938.

4. Because the Mosbach synagogue was enclosed by houses, the furnishings and Torah Scrolls were removed and burned in the square.
10 NOVEMBER 1938.

5. The synagogue of Laucheim was ravaged during the *Week of the Broken Glass* and then used as a stable.

Nürnberg Laws were essential to the enforcement of extreme antisemitic measures, such as revoking citizenship, eviction, deportation and ultimately, the destruction of the Jews.

Various Steps in Preparation for and the Execution of the
Endlösung
30 January 1933
 Hitler became Chancellor of the German Reich.
1 April 1933
 National boycott of Jewish shops and enterprises.
7 April 1933
 All Jewish officials were fired.
10 May 1933
 The books of Jewish and anti-Nazi writers were burned in public.
22 September 1933
 Reichkulturkammer was founded. Jews were barred from membership.
21 May 1935
 Jews were no longer drafted in the army.

Summer 1935
 Signs appeared everywhere: 'Jews are not welcome'.
26 April 1938
 Jews had to have their possessions registered.
23 July 1938
 Introduction of identity cards for Jews.
17 August 1938
 Jewish men had to add *'Israel'*, Jewish women, *'Sara'* to their first names.
5 October 1938
 Passports for Jews were stamped with a *'J'*.
28 October 1938
 17,000 Polish Jews were deported from Germany to Poland.
9-10 November 1938
 Pogrom against Jewish shops and synagogues, the so-called *'Reichskristallnacht'* (start of the Week of the Broken Glass). About 30,000 Jews were deported to camps.
15 November 1938
 Jewish children were only allowed to attend Jewish schools.

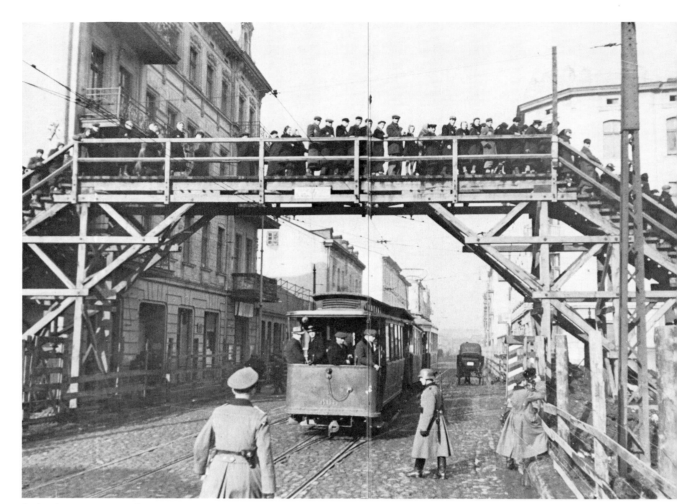

6. An *Aryan* street running straight through the ghetto of Lodz, Poland, so that Jews had to use a footbridge.

7. Austrian Jews with the yellow star.
VIENNA. 1941.

13 December 1938

Regulation about the confiscation of Jewish enterprises.

1 September 1939

The Second World War began with the German attack on Poland.

September 1939

SS and Wehrmacht (army) pogroms in Poland.

12 October 1939

First deportations of Jews from Austria to Poland.

28 October 1939

The first regulation about wearing yellow stars, Wloclawek, Poland.

30 April 1940

First ghetto established in Lodz, Poland.

31 July 1941

Göring assigned the deportation of European Jews to Heydrich: the start of the 'Endlösung'.

23 September 1941

First experimental gassing in Auschwitz, Poland.

December 1941

First permanent extermination camp established in Chelmno, Poland.

31 January 1942

The 'Einsatzgruppe A' (execution squad) reported having murdered 229,052 Jews in the Baltic countries.

18 May 1942

Extermination camp established in Sobibor, Poland.

23 June 1942

First selection for the gas chambers in Auschwitz-Birkenau.

1942-1943-1944

Millions of Jews from the occupied areas were deported to the extermination champs.

End October 1944

Last gassing in Auschwitz-Birkenau.

9. Jews from the ghetto in Marysin, Poland, on their way to the extermination camps.
AUGUST 1944.

8. Mass execution by an *Einsatzgruppe* (Execution squad).

Chapter 13

Shoah

'There were not six million Jews murdered,
one was murdered,
six million times.'
(Abel Herzberg)

The World Remained Silent

Elie Wiesel wrote: *'And yet the civilized world knew it; and the civilized world remained silent. But where was man in all that? And how was it possible that our spiritual civilization resulted in that? All the religious leaders, all the thinkers, all those philosophers so passionate about the truth, all those professors of morality drunk on justice: how can their lessons in ethics be related to Mengele, the big boss of the selections in Auschwitz? I did not find the answer. I told myself that somewhere a terribly serious mistake must have been made, but I did not know what mistake, or by whom. When and where had history taken a turn for the worse? I remember words spoken by a young Talmudist with the appearance of an old man, my comrade at work, who carried rocks with me that were heavier than ourselves: "We have to admit", he muttered, "we have to admit that our people did not pass the Law to other nations; let us forget Abraham and the example he gave; Moses and his justice, the prophets and their message; our contribution to philosophy, the sciences, literature, let us imagine that all of that is unimportant or that it did not even exist. Maimonides, Nachmanides, Rashi: nothing. Spinoza, Bergson, Einstein, Freud: nothing. Imagine that we contributed nothing to progress, nothing to the benefit of mankind. But about one thing we can not be challenged: the hoodlums, the mass murderers of history – the Pharaohs, the Neros, the Khmelnitskis, the Hitlers – they are not to be found among us."*

That brings us back to our starting point: the relation between Jews and Christians. In all the turmoil, this relationship must be reconsidered. Because a new truth struck us: when the victims were all Jews, the murderers were all Christians. What explanation is there that a Hitler or a Himmler was never excommunicated by the Pope? That Pope Pius XII never considered it urgent, or even necessary, to condemn Auschwitz? That in the SS there was a high percentage of Christians who remained devoted to their Christian tradition until the end? That certain murderers went to confession between murders? And that all of them came from Christian families and had enjoyed a Christian upbringing? How can it be explained that being Christian did not make their hands tremble when they shot down children, nor their consciences rebel when they drove naked and battered victims into the factories of death?'

Origin of the Estimated Six Million European Jews Killed

Soviet Union, Estonia	
Latvia, Lithuania	
Poland	4,566,000
Hungary	300,000
Czechoslovakia	277,000
Rumania	264,000
Germany	125,000
The Netherlands	106,000
France	83,000
Austria	70,000
Greece	65,000
Yugoslavia	60,000
Belgium	24,000
Italy	7,500
Norway	868
Luxemburg	700
Denmark	120

The entrance gate of
Auschwitz-Birkenau.

Chapter 14

Postwar Developments in Western Europe

When the Nazis had been defeated, it became clear what their antisemitism had led to: more than half of European Jewry had been murdered.

The shock was so great that for the first time in western history, the explicit expression of antisemitic attitudes became almost taboo.

A number of prominent Nazi figures were sentenced during the Nürnberg Trials: countless others who had played a role in the destruction went free. Except for some

incidents and the writings of marginal figures, relative calm prevailed until the Seventies. In November 1975, a majority of the United Nations supported a resolution in which Zionism was labelled *'a form of racism'*. Anti-Zionism, which rejected the right of Israel to exist as a Jewish state, increasingly posed as a new legitimization for hatred of Jews in those years. Not only the Israeli government, but often all Jews, even those outside Israel, were held responsible for Israel's acts. About 1980, there was a conspicuous outbreak of violence. In all the countries of Western Europe, there were actions against Jewish organizations and persons. There was also an increase in antisemitic threats and graffiti.

1. In September 1946, forty Jews fell victim to a pogrom in Kielce, Poland. A year after the end of the Second World War, an accusation of ritual murder was the cause of a number of pogroms in Poland.

Religious Reactions to the Shoah

The French philosopher Albert Camus once remarked: *'During the period of terror, I waited a long time to hear a powerful message from Rome. I, the unbeliever? Yes indeed, exactly. Because I knew that when confronted with tyranny, spiritual values are irretrievably lost if a louder voice does not speak out in condemnation. It is said that this voice did speak out. But I swear that I and millions of persons like me never heard it.'*

Pope Pius XII also remained silent after the Second World War. On 2 June 1945, he held a speech for the College of Cardinals in which he said that no one could reproach the Church for not having perceived the true character of the National Socialist movement in time, and pointing out how dangerous it was for Christian culture. In his speech he also recalled the bishops, priests and laity who had died as victims of the Nazi terror, but he did not say a word about the *'Endlösung'* of six million Jews. Auschwitz lay beyond this pope's field of vision; he stayed confined within the traditional thinking of the church about Jews.

On April 8 1948, the *Bruderrat der Evangelische Kirche* (Council of the Evangelical Church) published a declaration about the relation of the Church to the Jewish people. It concluded, saying literally: *'It is a sign of God's indulgence that God's judgement pursues the Jewish people in their rejection right up until today. The judgement on the Jewish people is the eternal confirmation of the (Christian) truth, of the reality of God's word, and finally, a warning to His community. The doom of the Jews is silent proof that God will not stand for any nonsense in warning us Christians and admonishing Jews.'*

2. Antisemitic graffiti on the memorial to the Jewish dead of the Hague. 1979.

3. Graffiti in the Jewish cemetary of Vienna. 1977.

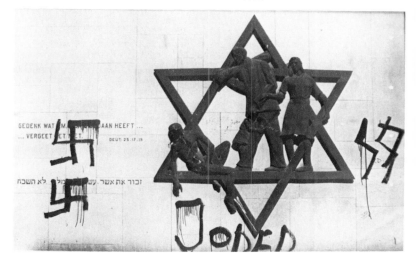

4. Hoveniersstraat in Antwerp after a bomb attack on the synagogue which killed two people. 1981.

The United Nations and the Equation of Zionism with Racism

On 10 November 1975, the United Nations General Assembly passed Resolution 3379, of which the final sentence reads: *'Zionism is a form of racism and of racial discrimination.'* The resolution was passed with 72 votes for, 35 votes against and 32 abstentions. Almost all the countries of Eastern Europe and the Third World voted for the resolution. Most western countries voted against it. A series of declarations with similar import from international forums preceded the decision of the United Nations. The Organization for African Unity declared in July 1975: *'The racist regime in occupied Palestine and the racist regime of Zimbabwe (formerly Rhodesia) and South Africa have a common imperialist origin. They form a unit ..., their politics serve to suppress human dignity and integrity.'*

Meeting in Mexico in July 1975, the International Conference of Women passed the following declaration: *'International cooperation and preservation of peace promotes the elimination of colonialism and no-colonialism, Zionism, apartheid and all forms of racial discrimination.'* The foreign ministers of the Non-Allied countries at a conference in August 1975 *'severely condemned (Zionism) as a danger to world peace and safety'* and called on all countries to *'resist this racist and imperialist ideology.'*

After 1975, the equation of Zionism with racism became a regular part of the declarations of international meetings.

Since 1982, the United Nations has held a yearly vote on Iran's motion to exclude Israel from the annual session. Israel's existence, according to the Iranian speaker, is: *'an expression of moral decay and the decay of human dignity'*. The PLO observer at the United Nations expressed surprise that the plenary session did not revoke the mandate of *'the Judaist-Nazi regime*

SOCIAL STUDIES TEACHER
LIVE OAK MIDDLE SCHOOL
2082 PENNINGTON RD
LIVE OAK CA 95953-2516

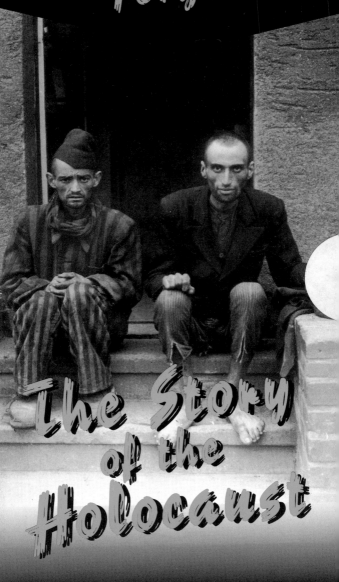

We Must Never Forget:

The Story of the Holocaust

ku
knowledge unlimited inc.

of Tel Aviv.' The Libyan representative supported Iran's motion: *'Israeli Nazism and its expansion are even more dangerous than Hitler's Nazism.'* Each year, the number of countries that support Iran's attempt to revoke the United Nations mandate for Israel has grown.

The equation of Zionism with racism also has an effect in various spheres outside the United Nations. Jewish organizations in Western Europe, for instance, were barred from participation in anti-racist symposiums with a wide range of constituents.

5. Four were dead and countless people were wounded in an attack on a synagogue in the Rue Copernic, Paris. OCTOBER 1980.

6. On 9 August 1982 two men sprayed the Jewish restaurant Goldenberg in Paris with machine gun fire, killing six, and wounding twenty-two.

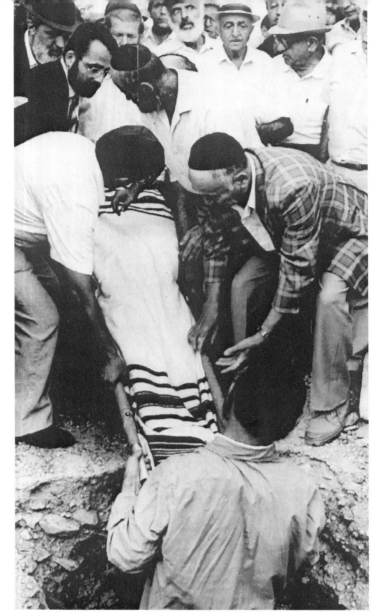

7. The funeral in Jerusalem of one of the victims of the attack on the synagogue in Istanbul. SEPTEMBER 1986.

RACISME
APARTHEID
ZIONISME
NOOIT

8. More than ten years after the resolution *Zionism is racism* was passed by the United Nations, a banner at the commemoration of the February Strike (an anti-Nazi strike for Jews in 1941).
AMSTERDAM 1988.

9. The interior of the Neve Shalom Synagogue in Istanbul after an attack which killed twenty-five people. SEPTEMBER 1986.

Chapter 15

Antisemitism and Anti-Zionism in the Arab World

Together with the Christians, the Jews in the Islamic countries formed a barely tolerated minority for centuries. They had to pay special taxes and were subjected to clothing regulations, but had greater religious and economic freedom than in the Christian world. With the arrival of the first Zionists in Palestine at the beginning of the twentieth century, this relationship began to change.

In the Thirties the Islamic leader in Palestine, the Grand Mufti of Jerusalem, regarded Hitler as an ally in his struggle against the Jewish colonists. One of the influences that resulted in a harsher Arab antisemitism was that of Nazi Germany.

In 1948, the state of Israel was founded. The Arab countries attacked Israel and lost the first Israeli-Arab war.

Jewish communities, present in the Arab world for hundreds of years, came to be regarded differently: as representatives of a Zionist aggressor. Arab antisemitism cannot be considered without taking the conflict between Israel and the surrounding countries into account.

Religious and social elements play minor roles; antisemitism is regarded as a political weapon in the fight against Israel. The enmity toward Israel, first directed toward Isrealis, has spread out toward Jews in general.

1. The rabbi of the Ifrane Synagogue in Morocco. Instead of a turban he is wearing the obligatory dotted cloth. C. 1950.

. The Grand Mufti of Je-   seini, visiting Adolf Hitler.
usalem, Haji Amin al-Hu-   OCTOBER 1941.

against the Jews of the entire world, dangerous enemies, whose secret arms are money, corruption and intrigues... Arab nationalism owes to Your Excellency a debt of gratitude and of recognition for having again and again brought up in ringing speeches the question of Palestine. I am anxious here to reiterate my thanks to Your Excellency and to assure Your Excellency of the sentiments of friendship, of sympathy, and of admiration, which the Arab people pledges to Your Excellency, great Führer, and to the courageous German people. I take this occasion to delegate to the German Government my private secretary in order to initiate in the name of the strongest and largest Arab organization and in my own name the negotiations necessary for sincere and loyal cooperation in all fields.'

The Grand Mufti of Jerusalem

In 1914, the periodical *Falastin* – with its extremist Arab nationalist slant – was abolished by the Ottoman authorities because of its racist hate propaganda. The periodical had agitated against the immigration of Jewish refugees from Russia. In the Twenties, the publication reappeared and led campaigns against Jewish immigration. As a result of anti-Jewish propaganda and terror, the British government took measures between the Twenties and the Forties to restrict Jewish immigration to Palestine. In 1921, an extremist, pan-Arab nationalist, Haji Amin al-Huseini, was appointed Grand Mufti of Jerusalem, a religious leader. Three weeks after his appointment, he led a pogrom in which forty-three Jews were murdered. From the beginning of the Second World War the Mufti led a rebellion of Iraqis, Syrians and Lebanese with support from Nazi Germany against the Allied Forces.

On 20 January 1941, the Mufti wrote to Hitler from Baghdad as follows: '*(Palestine) is a case of creating an obstacle to the unity and independence of the Arab countries by pitting them directly*

3. The devastated synagogue in Cairo after the pogrom in 1945.

In October 1941, the Mufti fled to Berlin where he met Hitler, who promised his support for the *solution of the Jewish problem* in Palestine. The Mufti supplied Radio Berlin with broadcasts in Arabic. In one of his radio speeches he said: *'Arabs, rise as one man and fight for your sacred rights. Kill the Jews wherever you find them. This pleases God, history and religion. This saves your honor. God is with you.'*

During the Nürnberg Trials, a highly ranking Nazi officer testified that the Mufti was one of the most vocal advocates of the total extermination of Jews. In 1947, the Mufti settled in Cairo, where he led attacks on Jewish communities and gave shelter to Nazi refugees.

4. The devastated Jewish cemetary of Damascus in the Sixties.

5. The book *World Zionism.* Egyptian state publication with *The Protocols of the Elders of Zion* as an appendix. 1956.

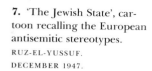

6. Arab edition of *Mein Kampf* circulated by the PLO in 1982.

7. 'The Jewish State', cartoon recalling the European antisemitic stereotypes.
RUZ-EL-YUSSUF.
DECEMBER 1947.

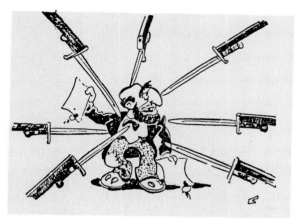

8. 'Instructions for the use of the Star of David.' This cartoon appeared during the June war of 1967 in Baghdad and Cairo.

9. From a Palestinian date book of 1975:'Adolf Hitler... the spiritual father of Israel.'

العماد

مصطفى طلاس

فطير صهيون

10. The Syrian Minister of Defense Mustafa Tlas wrote a book *The Matzoh of Zion* (1983), in which for the umpteenth time ritual murder was cited.

Arab Antisemitism after the Foundation of Israel

In the session of November 1947, the United Nations decided to partition Palestine into an Arab and a Jewish state; there were thirty-three votes for, thirteen votes against, and ten

sition to the Jewish state originated partially in Islamic antisemitism and Pan-Arab nationalism and was displayed by the positive attitude of Arab leaders toward the Nazis from the Thirties.

Between 1945 and 1948, there were pogroms in Syria, Iraq, Egypt, Libya and Yemen, which cost hundreds of Jews their lives. After the foundation of the state of Israel in 1948, hundreds of thousands of Jews were driven out of Arab countries. In Syria, the whole Jewish community was held hostage. In 1952, Nasser, one of the associates of the Mufti, came to power in Egypt with his corps of pro-German Free Officers. He provided high governmental functions for the Nazis who had fled to the Middle East. In interviews he promoted the *Protocols of the Elders of Zion*. In December 1953, he declared: *'To the disaster of Palestine there is no parallel in human history'*. He said to a *New York Post* reporter in 1955: *'In am not fighting solely against Israel but also against world Zionism and Jewish capital.'*

Antisemitic propaganda was introduced in the media, education and culture, and supported by the governments in other Arab countries. The legend of the ritual murder was circulated in a number of articles, books and plays. In Beirut *The Barbarism of the Instructions of the Talmud* was published in 1968, a translation of August Röhling's *Talmudjude* of 1871. In 1985 a book appeared in Syria, *The Matzoh of Zion*, by Mustafa Tlas, the Syrian Minister of Defense. The Egyptian Ministry of Education had the book *Talmudic Sacrifices* republished in 1962, written by Habib Faris in 1890. In a preface the publisher wrote that the book was: *'...an explicit documentation of indictment, based upon clear-cut evidence that the Jewish people permit the shedding of blood as a religious duty enjoined in the Talmud.'*

11. After the hijacking of the *Achille Lauro*, passengers and crew examine the spot where the body of Leo Klinghofer was thrown overboard. Palestinian hijackers had murdered the American invalid because of his Jewish origin. OCTOBER 1985.

abstentions. The United Nations then recognized the state of Israel. The Arab League, a majority of which took no part in the voting, did not accept this partition. The foundation of the state of Israel was regarded as an impermissible assault on the Arabian character of the Arab world. Oppo-

Chapter 16

The Soviet Union and the Jews

In past centuries, the hatred of Jews was strongly incited by the Russian Orthodox Church, especially at Easter. At the end of the nineteenth century, pogroms occurred regularly – slaughters tolerated by the government – especially after socio-economic difficulties. The Revolution of 1917 condemned antisemitism and recognized the individual character of the Jewish minority, although it was almost impossible to implement this recognition. Decidedly antisemitic attitudes existed under Stalin.

This became clear in the so-called Doctors' Trials of 1953: Jewish doctors were imprisoned on false charges of poisoning.

In government propaganda against Israel and Zionism, regular use was made of the centuries of antisemitic imagery. Until the Eighties, it was almost impossible for Russian Jews to study Hebrew or to practice the Jewish religion. Immigration requests usually meant the start of a long tortuous process. There has seemed to be some improvement in the past few years through the new political course in the Soviet Union. *Glasnost* does, however, have some negative effects. Because widely varying opinions can now be voiced more openly, expression of antisemitism is increasing, as for instance in the ultra-nationalist *Pamjat* movement.

1. Cartoon about the so-called *Doctors Trial*: 'Proof of the Crime.' The Jew is unmasked. From the Russian magazine *Krokodil*. JANUARY 1953.

2. 'The Flag of Zionist Mob.' PRAVDA VOSTOKA. DECEMBER 1971.

Propaganda against Jews, Cosmopolitans and Zionists

Within the Bolshevist movement during the years of the Russian Revolution, the attitude prevailed that Judaism was a relic of the past, and had no future. The struggle for equal national rights for the Jews was thought of as an obstacle to class solidarity. It was assumed that the Jewish proletariat would dissolve into the working class. Once a proletarian dictatorship was established, antisemitism would also disappear. The emancipation granted the Jews as a result of the civil revolution of March 1917, was maintained after the Communist revolution in the same year. From the beginning of the Twenties, however, their rights were increasingly restricted: Hebrew, a *reactionary language*, was forbidden; Jewish organizations were abolished and Zionists were widely persecuted. At the same time, antisemitism was condemned. In

1926, Michail I. Kalinin, titular head of the Soviet Union, declared: '... *the Russian intelligentsia (is)... perhaps even more antisemitic today than it was under czarism.*' The policy of the state and party was actually in accordance with '*total annihilation of the Zionist hydra.*' Between 1936 and 1939, Stalin launched an intensive campaign against 'Zionist-imperialist suppression of the Palestinian Arabs.'

3. During the last five years of Stalin's regime (1948-53) Jews were persecuted elsewhere in the Eastern bloc, too. Rudolf Slánský, of Jewish origin and Secretary General of the Czechoslovakian Communist Party, was hanged with ten companions after a show trial.
DECEMBER 1952.

In the course of the Second World War, the international policy of the Soviet Union changed in favor of a Jewish state in Palestine. In 1947, the Soviet Union supported the foundation of the state of Israel. On the home front, however, Israel was denounced as a form of 'bourgeois Jewish nationalism.' Many Jewish intellectuals and artists were put on trial as 'cosmopolitans' during fierce campaigns. When the Soviet Union's sphere of influence in the Middle East did not expand in the wake of the support it gave to the state of Israel, the assault of Communist countries led by Moscow was redirected from its emphasis on Jews as cosmopolitans to Jews as Zionists. In 1952, show trials were conducted in Eastern European countries, in which Jewish Communists were sentenced to death as 'Zionist bourgeois-nationalist traitors of the people', and as 'conspirators against the state'.

In the Sixties, Zionists were portrayed as Nazi accomplices in various publications. After the Six Days' War in 1967, Zionists were equated to Nazis in propaganda. A state publishing house circulated the books: *Judaism and Zionism*, by T. Kichko in 1968, and *Look Out: Zionism*, by J. Ivanov in 1969. In these books, Jewish organizations and institutions were described as parts of an 'international Jewish conspiracy' and Judaism was portrayed as a religion which was said to '*summon its followers to the enslavement and genocide of all peoples.*'

4. 'The Tentacles of the Octopus'.
KROKODIL. 1972.

THE SOVIET UNION AND THE JEWS

5. Moscow citizens looking at the slogan 'To the grave with the Jews', graffiti opposite the house of a refusenik.
JUNE 1978.

6. 'The Newest Prayer'. The classical antisemitic portrayal of the avaricious Jew in a cartoon against Jewish activists.
VECHERNAYA MOSKVA. 1973.

The Pamjat Movement

In Russian nationalist circles a movement originated which began to manifest itself in the Eighties as an organization to preserve the traditional Russian cultural inheritance. In the period of *Glasnost*, this movement became publicly active under the names of *Pamjat* (Memory) and *Otechenstvo* (Fatherland). Characteristic of *Pamjat* publications is the *Appeal to the Russian People* of 1987: *Who would dare act against their own people? Only those who are remote from it and have not known its soul for a long time and are unable to understand it. It is they who are now trying to convince everyone that there are no dark forces in the state and no conspiracy. ... In whose hands are the mass media? ... We declare ourselves the political opposition to all the dark forces in the Party and the State! ... The battles ... are still to be fought! International Zionism and Freemasonry have removed their visor and gone openly on the offensive against the last remaining islets of spirituality and consciousness. ... The press, radio, and television are preaching cosmopolitism and idolatry towards the West, and excluding what is fundamentally national and belongs to the people. ... We, together with the people, demand that all forces be mobilized to explain the danger Zionism represents in our country and that an end be put to the actions of those who are selling their homeland for 30 pieces of silver! Stop the cosmopolites! ... We must revive the centuries-old institution of the ploughman. We must bring men back to the land! Down with giant cities! ... For our struggle is just*

7. Cartoon 'Israël'.
SOVJETSKAJA ROSSIA. OCTOBER 1982.

beginning. And this "Appeal" will find a response in your hearts and move you to action if you overcome your fear of physical violence ... To conclude our Appeal, we wish especially to emphasize that the Pamyat Patriotic Association has nothing in common with chauvinism, or antisemitism, or any other form of racial discrimination! ... We see cosmopolitism invading all that is national with the help of international Zionist capital. ... The enemy is he who believes that the problem of Zionism and Freemasonry is an idle invention! And so now we know the truth! Instead of plaintiffs, we must become fighters!'

8. Graves in the Jewish cemetary in Leningrad, destroyed on Adolf Hitler's birthday.
1987.

9. Demonstration of the ultra-nationalist and antisemitic *Pamjat* movement.
MOSCOW. 1987.

Chapter 17

Denying and Trying to Excuse the Mass Murder of Jews

The Nazi ideology did not disappear with the military defeat of Nazi Germany. In the mid-Seventies, political groups emerged in western countries which tried to win new supporters for Nazi ideas. They simply denied Nazi crimes, such as the slaughter of millions of Jews, and labelled them *Jewish lies*. Typical publications in this field were *The Hoax of the 20th Century* by the American, Arthur Butz; *Die Auschwitz-Lüge* ('The Auschwitz Lie') by the German Thies Christopherson; and *Did Six Million*

Really Die? by Richard Harwood, alias Richard Verrall of the *National Front* in England.

The French leader of the *Front National*, Le Pen after being convicted of antisemitism once, did not deny the mass murders but trivialized them, by calling them 'merely a detail.'

In extreme religious circles the idea is sometimes circulated that Jews themselves are to blame for Auschwitz because they do not accept Jesus.

A new element in anti-Jewish propaganda is the story that Zionists collaborated with the Nazis. The *Anti-Zionist committee of the Soviet Union* was the main source of this accusation at the beginning of the Eighties.

Myths of Denial

In 1948, the French fascist writer Maurice Bardèche published the book *Nuremberg ou la Terre Promise* ('Nürnberg or the Promised Land'). It was in Nürnberg in 1945-46 that the first trial against top ranking Nazis was held and that the scope of Nazi crimes and destruction were revealed.

Bardèche, however, titled his book and claimed: *'We Have Been Betrayed for Three Years.'* His book was a model for countless others which denied the Nazi crimes. According to him, the victors falsified history in Nürnberg. The truth, as Bardèche saw it, was that the war crimes and atrocities had been committed by the Allies, while Germany had waged a merely defensive war. He believed photos of concentration camps, proof of the crimes, were *'too good to be true'*, that deaths were the result of food shortages and epidemics, and that gas was solely used as a *'disinfectant'*. According to Bardèche, The *Final Solution of the Jewish Problem* meant the establishment of ghettos in the East. It was not right to sympathize with Jews, either, because they were the cause of the war. Bardèche's reasoning was adopted by the Frenchman Paul Rassinier, a postwar Socialist member of parliament who had been deported to the camps Buchenwald and Dora for taking part in the Resistance during the Nazi occupation.

2. Demonstration of the German *Aktionsgruppe Nationaler Sozialisten*: 'Jackass that I am, I still believe that Jews were gassed in German camps.'
HAMBURG. MAY 1978.

3. Cover of *Did Six Million Really Die?* written by Richard Verrall of the *National Front* in England.
C. 1977.

Historical Fact No. 1

DID SIX MILLION REALLY DIE?

THE TRUTH AT LAST

1. In September 1987, the leader of the *Front National* in France, le Pen, called the gas chambers 'merely a detail in the history of the Second World War'.

The writings of Bardèche and Rassinier were frequently cited in neo-Nazi publications, in which the destruction of Jews was denied in order or to rehabilitate Nazism. Rassinier was the mentor of the French linguist, Faurisson, whose writings received a great deal of publicity. In a series of publications after 1974, beginning with an interview for the satirical newspaper *Le Canard Enchaîné*, Faurisson dismissed the Holocaust as a fabrication, denied the existence of gas chambers, and attacked the Diary of Anne Frank as a forgery. In ex-

tremist publications in America and England, the denial of the mass murder of Jews has been mixed with anti-Zionism for years: *'Further, we assert that the "Holocaust" lie was perpetrated by Zionist-Jewry's stunning propaganda machine for the purpose of filling the minds of Gentile people the world over with such guilt feelings ... Israel could not have been created in 1948, nor could it have survived since then, without the ability of Zionist agencies to exert financial, political and moral blackmail against the Gentile world as a result of never-ending "Holocaust" propaganda.'*

4. Sticker of the American Institute for Historical Review.
C. 1984.

NAZI GASSINGS A MYTH?
A New Look at The Holocaust
Send a self-addressed envelope with 37 cents postage for the incredible story of a genocide that never was
Institute for Historical Review • P.O. Box 1306 • Torrance, Calif. 90505

5. In neo-Nazi periodicals there is a lot of publicity for Butz's book.

6. In this French publication the trial of war criminal Barbie is dismissed as 'Shoah-business.'
1988.

7. Cartoon from the American press. The expulsion of fifteen Palestinians by Israel is equated with the deportations to the gas chambers.
BEGINNING OF 1988.

Zijn bloed kome over ons en over onze kinderen!

9. 'Jews are Nazis'. Banner in a demonstration in London for solidarity with the Palestinians.
1988.

8. Pamphlet of the Dutch evangelist couple Goeree. They claim that the centuries of persecution of Jews is punishment for their denial of Jesus.

Equation of Zionism with Nazism in the Soviet Union

From the early Seventies on, Zionism was equated with Nazism and Zionists were accused of collaboration with Nazi Germany in official publications in the Soviet Union and in other east European countries. A staff member of the Russian Academy of Science, Lev Kornejev, in his book *The Class Character of Zionism* (1982), wrote: '*If there had been no Zionist-Nazipact, the number of victims of the Second World War would naturally have been smaller.*'

His book was favorably discussed in the government newspaper and in party publications. The union newspaper *Rabochaja Gazeta* added: '*Israel applies the same methods which were first tested once upon a time by the Gauleiters of the Third Reich. ... The Zionists succeeded for a long time in hiding from the world their criminal connections with Hitlerite Fascism. ... Several dozen former SS officers, former pupils of the Hitler-Jugend (Hitler Youth) taught in Israeli para-military school camps and prepared specialists in conducting punitive expeditions.*' (Kiev, 11 February 1983)

Chapter 18

Coping with the Difficult Past

In past years, there have been a number of emotional debates not directly concerned with antisemitism but rather with the way in which society copes with the Shoah, the mass murder of Jews. In the Federal Republic of Germany, for instance, in government circles as well, there has recently been a visible tendency to lump together all the dead of the Second World War, regardless of whether they were killed as soldiers, murdered in death camps, or died as civilian victims. The visit Kohl and Reagan paid to Bitburg in May 1985 was part of this trend. Many people fear that the specific nature of the Shoah, stemming from a long tradition of antisemitism, will simply be suppressed in the near future.

When people of prominence refuse to acknowledge their own responsibility, or their own involvement in the difficult past, emotions run particularly high. An obvious example of this is the Waldheim affair. Waldheim called his military service under the Nazi regime '*only doing my duty*', even though the criminal nature of that regime was no secret after 1940. Protests from the Jewish community against such an extremely insensitive attitude usually end in manifestations of antisemitism – with the messenger being condemned for the bad tidings he brings.

For the churches, discussion of their involvement in and their share of responsibility for the centuries-long tradition of antisemitism is difficult. Only very recently has there been any self-criticism within the Roman Catholic Church.

1. Protest against Waldheim: 'Do your duty, resign'.
VIENNA. BEGINNING OF 1988.

Elie Wiesel on Babi-Jar

'Babi-Jar or the suffering of the Jews. Babi-Jar or the memory of the Jews or the fury of the Jews. I have never felt such fury and powerlessness. I still remember, I shall always remember. It was in 1965. I was there for the first time. I walked through Kiev in search of the spot where, between Rosh Hashana and Yom Kippur in 1941, the German murderers killed fifty to eighty thousand Jews ... But at that moment, looking at the landscape of Babi-Jar, I felt only fury rising in me: fury too at the regime that despite foreign pressure in 1965 gave no permission to erect a monument in memory of the victims devoured by hate and indifference. To me it was appalling that there was no tombstone, no inscription.

I returned to Kiev in August 1979. Official representatives of the town council felt they could now pat themselves on the back: a monument in Babi-Jar? Just look, there it was! And there it was indeed: a colossal and powerful memorial, such as only the Soviets can make. Impressive in every way except ... except that the word 'Jew' was not on it. This monument is regarded as having been erected in memory of Russian citizens, murdered by the Fascists ... Then I was angrier than I have ever been. In my speech I said exactly what I felt: 'In 1965 I stood in the same place and felt indignant; what I feel now is shame: I am ashamed for you ... you know very well that the men and women lying buried in this grave were murdered because they were Jews! What right have you to rob them of their identity? They lived as Jews, worked as Jews, they loved as Jews, they dreamed Jewish dreams and as Jews they were isolated and turned over to the executioner; because they were Jews they underwent fear, torture and death: what right do you now have to thrust them back into anonymity? On which grounds do you mutilate their very being? Why do you not give them justice posthumously, assign the place to them which they claimed in Jewish history with their lives?' Visibly embarrassed, the Russian officials and commentators tried to discuss, to explain, to justify themselves. To no avail. All the members of our delegation, Jews and Gentiles, responded with indignation. The memorial of Babi-Jar is a scandal. This is still another betrayal of the dead. If we reacted in this way, that is because, alas, Babi-Jar is not unique; on the contrary, it reflects a sort of current, the spirit of the times. Deserted in life, in memory the Jews of Babi-Jar are betrayed. Therefore the dull fury in us. And the endless sorrow.'

3. Pope John Paul II visiting Auschwitz, June 1979. He did not mention the role the Church played in two thousand years of antisemitism.

John Paul II

In Poland in June 1979, Pope John Paul II visited the death camp Auschwitz where he knelt in front of the stones commemorating the victims of Auschwitz and Birkenau. He said: *'I kneel on te Golgotha of the modern world, on these graves I kneel before all these inscriptions which bear the memories of the victims of Auschwitz.'* The Pope cited the inscriptions: Polish, English, Czech, Yiddish, Hebrew, and so forth. He said: *'I want to pause, in particular, at the inscription in Hebrew. This inscription commemorates the people whose sons and daughters were destined for complete destruction. This people began with Abraham, who is the father of our faith. This people who received the commandment "Thou shalt not kill" from God, has itself experienced in a special way what killing is.*

No one may ignore this inscription.'

Despite expressing appreciation for what he said, Jews and Christians were also confounded, because he did not say a word about the Catholic Church's complicity and guilt in regard to Auschwitz.

When on 13 April 1986 the Pope visited the synagogue in Rome, Chief Rabbi Elio Toaff referred to the complicity of the Church in persecuting Jews during the past centuries. John Paul II did condemn antisemitism in his speech – *'regardless of when and by whom it was practiced'* – but again he said nothing about the Church's role.

In Vienna, meeting with representatives of the Jewish community on the morning of 24 June 1988, during his visit to Austria, he said: *'The memories of the Shoah – the murder of millions of Jews in the death camps – continues to weigh heavily on you and on us, too. It would be unjust and incorrect, however, to lay the responsibility for these unspeakable crimes on Christianity. Then a world without God and in rebellion against Him revealed its horrible face, in the wish not only to destroy the Jewish people but also the faith of people who honor the Jew, Jesus of Nazareth, as the Savior of the world.'*

When the Pope visited the concentration camp Mauthausen in the afternoon, in a long speech he condemned the *'mad ideologies based on hatred and contempt for fellow human beings'* and he asked his audience not to forget the victims too quickly. However, he neglected to call Fascism by its name, to cite the Jewish victims, and most important of all, to condemn the offenders and accessories. In respect to both speeches the Pope made in Austria, Rabbi Eissenberg said: *'I still want you to know that we are very unhappy about these speeches, yes, even angry. The only Jew mentioned in the text is Jesus Christ and he was not killed in Mauthausen.'*

4. Chancellor Kohl and President Reagan visiting the German war cemetary in Bitburg together, forty years after the military defeat of the Nazis.
MAY 1985.

5. Protest against the visit to Bitburg: 'Why, Mr. President, are you visiting a cemetery where members of the SS are buried?'
MAY 1985.

Antisemitism in Austria: the Waldheim Affair

Kurt Waldheim, former Secretary General of the United Nations, decided to become a candidate for the presidency of Austria in 1986. The dull election campaign suddenly became international news when the World Jewish Congress disclosed Waldheim's war record. During the Second World War, Waldheim was a German officer, active in the Balkans, near Salonica, at a time when tens of thousands of Jews from Salonica were deported to the gas chambers in Auschwitz. Waldheim stated that he knew nothing about this; he had not mentioned it in his autobiography because he had forgotten all about it. The disclosures of the World Jewish Congress led to unusually fierce outbursts of antisemitism in Austria. It was not Waldheim and his war record which were attacked, but *the Jews*. Austria was portrayed as the defenseless little victim of *world Jewry*.

Waldheim eagerly participated in this: on 3 May 1986, the day before the first round of elections, a reporter from the French newspaper *Le Monde* asked him why the international press was so critical of him. Waldheim replied: '*Because it is dominated by the World Jewish Congress, as everyone knows*'.

The biggest newspaper in Austria, the *Neue Kronen-Zeitung*, spoke of a '*Jewish witch hunt*' and published a cover article titled '*The Power of the Jews*'. When in an Israeli newspaper an article appeared about the affair which displeased a Catholic politician from Salzburg, he imperiously demanded that the Jewish community in Vienna publicly repudiate the article or relations between 'Austrians and the Jewish people' would be endangered.

The deputy burgomaster of Linz, Dr. Carl Hödl, member of the Catholic Österreichische Volkspartei, proved how persistent antisemitic attitudes were. He wrote to the chairman of the World Jewish Congress: '*Your accusations against Waldheim must be evaluated just like those of others of your faith who condemned Jesus Christ to death two thousand years ago because he didn't fit in with the way the masters in Jerusalem thought.*' The old accusation of the murder of God was used again. Waldheim was elected president, but was shunned in international diplomatic relations. Ronald Lauder, who was appointed the American ambassador in 1988, did not visit him immediately as was customary. The *Salzburger Volkszeitung* knew the reason: because '*his grandfather had been a kosher emigrant from Europe, in search of the Promised land. Should the U.S. ambassador to Austria represent the interests of the United States or those of the inflammatory lobby of a powerful ethnic group?*'

6. Carl Hödl, deputy-burgomaster of Linz, who compared the protests of Jewish organizations against Waldheim to the Crucifixion of Jesus Christ.

7. President Kurt Waldheim being interviewed by the American journalist Pierre Salinger. Waldheim dismissed his record as a German officer in the army of occupation in the Balkans as '... only doing my duty'.
VIENNA. FEBRUARY 1988.

8. Support for Waldheim in a publication of the Fatah Revolutionary Council: 'Waldheim's victory is a slap in the face for the Zionist movement and its racist state.'
JUNE 1986.

Chapter 19

Developments in the Nineties

At the end of the Eighties great political and social changes took place in Central and Eastern Europe. Berlin saw the fall of the Wall which eventually led to the reunification of Germany. There were open protests against the Communist regimes in the Soviet Union's sa-tellite states. With the disintegration of the Soviet Union and the end of state Communism, years of suppressed nationalistic feelings surfaced again. While in the summer of 1991 the Commonwealth of Independent States was created from the Soviet Union, Yugoslavia became engaged in civil war. Nationalism is one of the most powerful forces in present-day Europe.

1. Berlin, the Brandenburg Gate, 25 December 1992. A human chain of light protesting against racism and the hatred of foreigners. There were mass demonstrations throughout Germany that winter in which millions of people participated.

All these developments also have an effect on antisemitism. Right-wing extremist groups in a number of Western European countries extend their hatred of foreigners and asylum-seekers to Jews as well. Even where there is hardly a Jewish section of the population left, as in Poland, we see virulent antisemitism. In Russia propaganda is circulated openly and on a large scale that is in no way less than the Nazi publication *Der Stürmer*. The revisionists, denying that the Holocaust took place, are still voicing their views, too.

Nevertheless, there are still a few glimmers of hope. In Germany, for example, the voices of increasing numbers of citizens are being raised against racial hatred and antisemitism in reaction to the excesses which are sometimes horrible. In Italy, too, thousands turned out in November 1992, many of them out of solidarity wearing the star of David; they were protesting the provocations and violent activities of Nazi skinheads against Jews.

After the fall of the Soviet Union

The new freedom of expression, still an unfamiliar phenomenon for many Soviet citizens after seventy years of Communism, is being abused by individuals and organizations to dust off old, long suppressed images of the enemy. Great political tensions and apparently insoluble socio-economic problems form an almost ideal breeding-ground for propaganda, which evokes one of the most persistent forms of prejudice and discrimination: antisemitism.

At this moment a great deal of antisemitic literature is openly on sale in the Moscow streets and subways. Every issue of one of the most popular periodicals, *Dej*, contains at least one ar-

2. The struggle between Ilya Muromez (the Russian national hero) and the 'Big Jew' (as the personification of evil). Illustration from the *Pamyat* periodical, February 1992.

ticle in which Jews are pointed to as being guilty of some evil or other. Antisemitic political organizations such as *Pamyat*, which have also become known through the Western media, form no more than the tip of the iceberg. A strong undercurrent of an antisemitic range of thought can be recognized even in so-called moderate nationalistic organizations.

The current propaganda is given all the more chance to flourish because in the former Soviet Union a process of self-criticism in regard to the antisemitic tradition never took place. In publications of patriotic movements, Jews are accused of being bent on the destruction of the Russian culture. Caricatures can be seen that literally seem to be adopted from the Nazi publication *Der Stürmer*. Moreover, age old Russian traditions are elaborated on, such as folk tales having antisemitic motifs. The folk tale about the struggle between the Russian national hero Ilya Muromez and the Big Jew, a personification of evil, was recently printed in installments in the *Pamyat* periodical.

Antisemitic attitudes are also met with among the intelligentsia. In 1991 an interview appeared in the *New York Times* with Valentin Rasputin, a prominent and very popular Russian writer. Rasputin said: 'The Russian Jews should feel responsible for the sin of the Russian Revolution, and for the forms it took. They should feel responsible for the terror during and especially after the Revolution. They played an important role and their guilt is great – for that as well as for the murder of God.'

Poland and Jews

Many people are amazed by current expressions of antisemitism in Poland; there are hardly any Jews still left in Poland.

Besides the 'classical' antisemitism (someone is no good *because* he or she is Jewish) we also see a new phenomenon in Poland: someone is no good, so he or she *must* be Jewish. Adam Michnik, an important member of 'Solidarity,' calls this 'magical antisemitism.' During Lech Walesa's election campaign in 1991, this phenomenon was manifested in a bitter way. The presidential candidate Tadeusz Mazowiecki, who was responsible for the policy of economizing and reform, was portrayed by his political opponents as a Jew. The word 'Jew' was the superlative form of the word 'scoundrel.' Mazowiecki was no longer any good, and he was therefore a Jew. During the campaign, slogans were scrawled, such as 'Gas the Jews' and 'Ship the Jews to Madagascar.'

When, after being elected president, Lech Walesa paid a visit to Israel and asked forgiveness for what Poland had done to the Jewish people, this statement aroused a wave of protest in the Polish press: 'This visit is an outrage. How can he ask Jews to forgive Poland?' (*Gazeta Wyborcza*, 4 June 1991)

Relations between the Catholic Church in Poland and Jews are still very strained. On 14 July 1989 Rabbi Weiss from New York, along with a group of Jews, protested on the grounds of Auschwitz against the presence of a convent on the spot where the poison gas Zyklon B had formerly been stored. Several demonstrators tried to force their way inside, but Polish workers doused them with pails of water. The visit was a protest against not keeping the promise to move the convent elsewhere. Only after years of worldwide protests was the Vatican prepared to compel the Polish diocese to keep its promise.

3. Rabbi Abraham Weiss of New York being doused at his public protest against the presence of the convent in Auschwitz, 14 July 1989.

When Cardinal Glemp spoke to a crowd of thousands of Catholics in August 1989, he also addressed the Jews, saying: *'Your power in the world is founded on the media which in various countries is entirely at your disposal. Don't use that power for anti-Polanism. If there were no anti-Polanism, there would also be no antisemitism in our country.'* Many were alarmed by the silence that followed the Cardinal's antisemitic remarks.

Germany after unification

The euphoria about German unification ended abruptly. Not only were the economic problems much greater than foreseen. What mainly led to great unrest was a number of antisemitic incidents and violence against asylum-seekers.

In the former German Democratic Republic (East Germany) the myth was always maintained that after 1945 all the good Germans could be found on this side of the border, and all the bad ones (for bad, read: ex-Nazis) on the other side. Any joint responsibility for Nazi crimes was denied, and no reparations were paid. No real education about Germany's National-Socialist past was given. On the sites of former concentration camps in East Germany, rallies were organized for the self-glorification of the anti-Fascist state.

The government stated that antisemitism was rooted out once and for all. When young people of the extreme right-wing began swinging bicycle chains at a 1989 punk concert and shouted: 'Jews get out', the East German authorities interpreted these shows of antisemitism as 'Western import.'

After unification, West-German Neo-Nazi groups seized the opportunity to launch a tremendous propaganda offensive. They profited from the fact that for a great many young people of

the former East Germany, the concept 'Fascist' had become an honorary title. The fatal attacks on foreigners and asylum-seekers have led to fierce reactions inside and outside Germany. Rostock and Mölln have become household words. And, within the small community of German Jews fear has also increased. Bombing the monument to the memory of the Jews of Berlin on 1 September 1992, and setting fire to the Jewish barrack in the former camp of Sachsenhausen a month later, have contributed to this fear.

A positive point, however, is that years of discussions about the German past in the media and in education have not been without result. In the winter of 1992-1993, millions of people have taken part in demonstrations against right-wing extremism. Partly due to this, the German government has forbidden a number of Neo-Nazi groups.

4. Cover of the French weekly, *Minute la France*, November 1992. The periodical is closely allied to Le Pen's Front National. The text next to the antisemitic caricature of the French Socialist Party leader reads: 'The end of Fabius.'

Antisemitism in a growing political party

In Belgium the extreme right-wing Vlaams Blok (Flemish Block) received the support of ten per cent of the voters in Flanders in the 1991 national elections, thus winning 18 seats in parliament.

What is striking about this party is that among its supporters there are a substantial number of persons who express their antisemitic attitudes in public, and in doing so, encounter no problems, either with the party or with Belgian justice. A good example of this is Jos Rogiers, until the end of 1991, editor-in-chief of the leading newspaper syndicate *De Standard/Het Nieuwsblad*. Rogiers led a local list of candidates for the Vlaams Blok and was also the author of the brochure, *The Holocaust Deception*, published in 1990 by the so-called 'Free Historical Research' group. In this brochure, Rogiers makes no secret of his Nazi sympathies. Shortly afterwards he published *'The Chosen Problem-People – The Jews as the fathers of Nazism, instigators of World War II, racial mass murderers and threat to the world.'* Rogiers had to leave *De Standard*, but was retained as a member of the Vlaams Blok.

That is not surprising either, if we look closely at the former activities of Karel Dillen, member of parliament for the Vlaams Blok. In 1952 he translated Maurice Bardèche's *'Nürnberg or the Promised Land'*, one of the standard works of revisionist literature, into Dutch, and he has never renounced that. The present leader of the Vlaams Blok, Filip Dewinter, was chairman of the Nationalistic Student Association (NSV) at the beginning of the Eighties. The antisemitism is undisguised in the NSV song: *'A dirty Jew ... we'll lay his bones bare, no flesh, no hair.'*

It is alarming that the support for the Vlaams Blok still seems to be increasing. There is a chance that the Party will dominate city policy in Antwerp, with its large Jewish community, after the elections for the city council in 1994.

5. Election propaganda of the Flemish Block: 'Our own people first...' The cartoon makes clear their views concerning who belongs and who does not.

Bibliography

Aanklacht tegen de leiding van een staatsvijandig samenzweerders-centrum met aan het hoofd Rudolf Slánský, **Proces in Praag van 20-27 nov. 1952,** Amsterdam 1953.

Adam, Uwe Dietrich,
Judenpolitik im Dritten Reich, Düsseldorf 1972.
Agobart of Lyons,
'De iudaicis superstitionibus' in: **Patrologia Latina** 104, 77-100.
Almog, Shmuel,
Antisemitism through the Ages, Oxford 1988.
Alon, Dafna,
Arab Racialism, Jerusalem 1969.
Andel, C.P., van,
Jodenhaat en Jodenangst. Over meer dan twintig eeuwen antisemitisme, Amersfoort 1983.
Anderson, George, K.,
The Legend of the Wandering Jew, Rhode Island 1965.
Ambrosius,
'Ninetyone Letters' in: **Patrologia Latina** 42.
Arkel, Dik van,
'De groei van het anti-Joodse stereotype. Een poging tot een hypothetisch-deductieve werkwijze in historisch onderzoek' in: **Tijdschrift voor sociale geschiedenis,** 1984, 34-68.
Auf der Mauer, H.J.,
'De paaspreek van Melito van Sardes. Joodse wortels. Christelijke her-interpretatie en anti-Joodse polemiek' in: L.A.R. Bakker/ H.P.M. Goddijn, **Joden en christenen. Een moeizaam gesprek door de eeuwen heen,** Baarn 1985, 64-80.
Augustine,
'Tractatus adversus iudaeos' in: **Patrologia Latina** 42.

Baroja, Julio Caro,
Los Judios en la Espana moderna y contemporanea, Madrid 1961.
Ben-Sassoon, H.H.,
A history of the Jewish People, Cambridge 1976.
Benz, Wolfgang,
Die Juden in Deutschland 1933-1945. Leben unter national-sozialistischer Herrschaft, München 1989.
Blumenkranz, Bernhard,
Histoire des Juifs en France, Toulouse 1972.
Juden und Judentum in der mittelalterlichen Kunst, Stuttgart 1965.
Brearley, Margaret,
'Hitler and Wagner', in: **Patterns of Prejudice,** 22 (1988) 3-22.
Broder, Henryk,
Der ewige Antisemit, Frankfurt 1986.
Bunzl, John and Marin, Bernd,
Antisemitismus in Oesterreich. So-zialhistorische und soziologische **Studien,** Innsbruck 1983.

Charlemagne,
'Capitularia de iudaeis' in: **Monumenta Germaniae Historica I,** 258-259.
Chrysostom, John,
'Eight sermons against the Jews' in: **Patrologia Graeca** 48, 483-942.
Cohn, Norman,
Warrant for genocide: The Myth of the World-Jewish Conspiracy and the Protocols of the Elders of Zion, London 1967.
Histoire d'un mythe. La 'conspiration' juive et les Protocoles des Sages de Sion Paris 1967.
Comay, Joan,
The Diaspora Story. The Epic of the Jewish People among the Nations, Jerusalem 1981.
Cooper, Abraham,
Portraits of Infamy, Los Angeles 1987.

Dawidowicz, Lucy,
The War against the Jews 1933-1945, New York 1977.
Denzler, Georg and Fabricius, Volker,
Die Kirchen im Dritten Reich. Band I: Darstellung, Band II: Dokumente, Frankfurt 1984.
Dobroszycki, Lucjan,
The Chronicle of the Lodz Ghetto 1941-1944, New Haven/London 1984.
Documents,
'Pamjat': 'An Appeal to the Russian People' in: **Soviet Jewish Affairs,** Vol. 18, Nr. 1, 1988.
Dubnow, Simon,
Die Geschichte des jüdischen Volkes in der Neuzeit. Das XVI. und die erste Hälfte des XVII. Jahrhunderts, Berlin 1927.

Eban, Abba,
Heritage. Civilization and the Jews, London 1964.
Eckert, W.P., Ehrlich E.L.,
Judenhass - Schuld der Christen?, Essen 1964.
Eckhart, Dietrich,
Der Bolschewismus von Moses bis Lenin. Zwei Gespräche zwischen Adolf Hitler und mir, München 1924.
Encyclopaedia Judaica, volume 3, Jerusalem 1974.
Encyclopaedia Judaica, Yearbook 1983/5, Jerusalem 1985.
Engelmann, Hans,
Kirche am Abgrund. Adolf Stöcker und seine anti-jüdische Bewegung, Berlin 1984.
Ericksen, Robert, P.,
Theologians under Hitler: Gerhard Kittel, Paul Althaus and Emanuel Hirsch, New Haven/London 1985.
Eschwege, Helmut,
Kennzeichen 'J'. Bilder, Dokumente,Berichte zur Geschichte der Verbrechen des Hitlerfaschismus an den deutschen Juden 1933-1945, Berlin 1966.

Flaiano, Ennio,
L'Opera completa di Paolo Uccello, Milano 1971.
Flannery, Edward, H.,
The Anguish of the Jews. Twenty-Three Centuries of Antisemitism, Mahwah/New York 1985.
Flusser, David,
Tussen oorsprong en schisma, Hilversum 1984.
Fornari, Salvatore,
La Roma del Ghetto, Roma 1984.
Fricke, Weddig,
Standrechtlich gekreuzigt. Prozess Jesu, Frankfurt 1987.
Fritzsch, Robert,
Nürnberg unterm Hakenkreuz im Dritten Reich 1933-1939, Düsseldorf 1983.
Fuchs, Eduard,
Die Juden in der Karikatur. Ein Beitrag zur Kulturgeschichte, München 1921.

Gager, John G.,
The Origins of Anti-Semitism: Attitudes Towards Judaism in Pagan and Christian Antiquity, New York 1983.
Geller, Henryk and Geller, Ruth,
Roma ebraica. Duemila anni di storia in immagini, Roma 1984.
Gielen, J.F.,
De wandelende Jood in volkskunde en letterkunde, Amsterdam 1931.
Gilbert, Martin,
Atlas of the Holocaust, Jerusalem 1982.
Jerusalem, Illustrated History Atlas, London 1977.
Jewish History Atlas, London 1976,
Goff, Jacques, Le,
La bourse et la vie: Economie et Religion au Moyen Age, Paris 1986.
Graml, Hermann,
Reichskristallnacht. Antisemitismus und Judenverfolgung im Dritten Reich, München 1988.
Gummersbach, Hans, W.,
Der Weg nach Auschwitz begann auch in Ahlen, Ahlen 1988.

Haddad, Mohanna en Yousuf, Salim,
Arab Perspectives of Judaism. A Study of image in the writings of Muslim Arab Authors 1848-1978, Utrecht 1984 (dissertation).
Hahn, Joachim,
Synagogen in Baden-Würthemberg, Stuttgart 1987.
Haliczer, Stephen,
'The First Holocaust: the Inquisition and the Converted Jews of Spain and Portugal' in: **Inquisition and Society in Early Modern Europe,** London 1987, 7-19.
Harkabi, Yehoshafat,

Arab Attitudes towards Israel, New York 1972.

Heer, Friedrich,
Gottes erstes Liebe. 2000 Jahre Judentum und Christentum.
Genesis des Österreichischen Katholiken Adolf Hitler, München 1967.

Hennigsen, J.,
Professor Sombarts Forschungsergebnisse zur Judenfrage, Hamburg 1912.

Henrikson, Alf and Berg, Björn,
Oosthoeks Encyclopedie, Utrecht 1980.

Heuberger, Rachel and Krohn, Helga,
Hinaus aus dem Ghetto. Juden in Frankfurt am Main 1800-1950, Frankfurt 1988.

Hirsch, Rudolf and Schuder, Rosemarie,
Der Gelbe Fleck. Wurzeln und Wirkungen des Judenhasses in der Deutschen Geschichte, Köln 1988.

Historikerstreit,
Die Dokumentation der Kontroverse um die Einzigartigkeit der nationalsozialistischen Judenvernichtigung, München 1987.

Hitler, Adolf,
Mein Kampf, München 1925.

Ildefons of Toledo,
'De virginitate peretua sanctae Mariae adversus tres infideles' in: **Patrologia Latina** 96, 53-102.

Izvestia,
February 27, 1988.

Jansen, Hans,
Theologische en kerkelijke wortels van het antisemitisme. Den Haag 1981 (5th edition 1983)
Nieuwtestamentische wortels van het antisemitisme. Diagnose en therapie in geschiedenis van joden en christenen, Den Haag 1985
'Anti-joods lezen van Mattheüs 27:25 in geschiedenis van christendom (1)' in: **Literama** 20 (1986) 444-486 (= text of broadcasting programs).
'Anti-joods lezen van Mattheüs 27:25 in geschiedenis van christendom (2)' in: **Literama** 21 (1987) 281-305 (= text of broadcasting programs).

Jansma, G. e.o.,
Erasmus, de actualiteit van zijn denken, Zutphen 1986.

Jenk, Peter and Sellmeyer, Martina,
Stationen auf dem Weg nach Auschwitz, Osnabrück 1988.

Julian of Toledo,
'De comprobatio aetatis sextae' in: **Patrologia Latina** 96, 537-586.

Justinianus I,
'Corpus Iuris Civilis' in: **Patrologia Graeca** 86, 943-1152.

Katz, Jacob,
From Prejudice to Destruction. Anti-Semitism: 1700-1933, Cambridge 1980,
The Darker Side of Genius. Richard Wagner's Antisemitism, Waltham, Mass., 1986.

Keller, Ulrich,
The Warsaw Ghetto in Photographs, New York 1984.

Kisch, Guido,
Erasmus Stellung zu Juden und Judentum, Tübingen 1969.

Kleeblatt, Norman, L.,
The Dreyfus Affair, London 1987.

Kochan, Lionel,
The Jews in Soviet Russia since 1917, Oxford 1978.

Kölnische Gesellschaft für Christlich-Jüdische Zusammenarbeit,
100 Jahre Deutscher Rassismus, Köln 1988.

Kulturabteilung des Amtes der Burgenlandischen Landesregierung,
Judentum im Mittelalter, Burgenland 1978.

Kupisch, Karl,
Adolf Stoecker, Hofprediger und Volkstribun, Berlin 1970.

Kwiet, K.,
Van Jodenhoed tot Gele Ster, Bussum 1973.

Lange, Nicolaas, de,
Atlas van de joodse wereld, Amsterdam 1985.

Lewis, Bernhard,
Semites and Anti-Semites. An Inquiry into Conflict and Prejudice, London 1986,
'Race and Colour in Islam' in: **Encounter,** vol. XXXV Nr.2, 1970.

Littman, David,
'Jews under Muslim Rule in the Late Nineteenth Century' in: **The Wiener Library Bulletin** 1975, Vol. XXXVIII, Nr.35/36.

Luther, Martin,
'Von den Juden und ihren Lügen' in: **Weimarer Ausgabe** 53.

Ma'Oz, Moshe,
The Image of the Jews in Official Arab Literature and Communications Media, Jerusalem 1976.

Maccoby, Hyam,
Judaism on trial. Jewish-Christian Disputations in the Middle Ages, London 1982.

Mackenzie, Norman,
Geheimgesellschaften, Genf 1969.

Markisch, Shimon,
Erasmus and the Jews. With an Afterword by Arthur A. Cohen, London 1986.

Martini, Raymond,
Pugio fidei, edition Joseph Voisin, Paris 1651.

Martire, Gregory and Clark, Ruth,
Anti-Semitism in the United States: A study of Prejudice in the 1980's, New York 1982.

Massing, Paul, W.,
Vorgeschichte des politischen Antisemitismus, Frankfurt 1986.

Matheson, Peter,
The Third Reich and the Christian Churches, Scotland 1981.

Meer, Frits van and Mohrmann, Christine,
Bildatlas der frühchristlichen Welt, Gütersloh 1959.

Memmi, Albert,
Who is an Arab Jew?, Jerusalem 1975.

Michman, J.,
Met voorbedachten rade. Ideologie en uitvoering van de Endlösung der Judenfrage, Amsterdam 1987.

Moore, R.I.,
The Formation of a Persecuting Society, Oxford 1987.

Narkies, Bezalel,
Spiegel van de joodse beschaving, Utrecht/Antwerpen 1974.

Nettler, Ronald, L.,
Past Trials and Present Tribulations. A Muslim Fundamentalist's View of the Jews, Oxford 1987.

Oberman, Heiko, A.,
Wurzeln des Antisemitismus - Christenangst und Judenplage im Zeitalter von Humanismus und Reformation, Berlin 1981.

Parmentier, M.F.G.,
'Joodse oorsprongen van het Christendom' in: L.A.R. Bakker en H.P.M. Goddijn, **Joden en christenen. Een moeizaam gesprek door de eeuwen heen,** Baarn 1985. 40-64.

Pleticha, Heinrich,
Das Bild des Juden in der Volks- und Jugend-Literatur vom 18. Jahrhundert bis 1945, Würzburg 1985.

Po-chia Hsia,
The Myth of Ritual Murder, London 1988.

Poliakov, Léon,
Breviaire de la haine, Paris 1951.
Histoire de l'antisémitisme, Tome I, II édition Pluriel, Paris 1981.
Le mythe aryen, Paris 1971.

Potok, Chaim,
Wanderings. History of the Jews, London 1978.

Prolingheuer, Hans,
Wir sind in die Irre gegangen. Die Schuld der Kirche unterm Hakenkreuz, Köln 1987.

Pulzer, Peter,
The Rise of Political Anti-Semitism in Germany and Austria, revised edition, London 1988.

Quinley, Harold E. and Glock, Charles Y.,
Anti-Semitism in America, New Brunswick 1983.

Rafetseder, Hermann,
Bücherverbrennungen. Die öffentliche Hinrichtung von Schriften im historischen Wandel, Wien/Köln 1988
Remembering
for the Future. The Impact of the Holocaust and Genocide on Jews and Christians. Proceedings of an International Conference, Oxford and London 10-17 July 1988, Oxford 1989
(3250 pp.)
Röhm, Eberhard and Thierfelder, Jörg,
Evangelische Kirche zwischen Kreuz und Hakenkreuz, Stuttgart 1981.
Rovart, Marie-France,
Le mythe du juif errant dans l'Europe du XIXe siècle, Paris 1988.
Rosenstrauch, Hazel,
Aus Nachbarn wurden Juden. Ausgrenzung und Selbstbehauptung 1933-1942, Berlin 1988.
Rubens, Alfred,
A History of Jewish Costume, London 1975.
Ruether, Rosemary,
Faith and Fratricide: The theological roots of Anti-Semitism, New York 1974.

Sardes, Melito, of,
'Peri Pascha' in: **Sources chrétiennes** 123.
Schoenberner, Gerhard,
Der Gelbe Stern. Die Judenverfolgung in Europa 1933 bis 1945, München 1978.
Schoon, Simon,
'Zijn bloed over ons en onze kinderen' in: **Verkenning en Bezinning** 16 (1984) nr.4.
Seidel, Gill,
De ontkenning van de Holocaust. Antisemitisme, racisme en Nieuw rechts, Baarn/Den Haag 1988.
Seiferth, Wolfgang,
Synagoge und Kirche im Mittelalter, München 1964.
Showalter, Dennis, E.,
Little Man. What Now? Der Stürmer in the Weimar Republic, Hamden Conn. 1982.
Smelik, Klaas,
Hagar en Sara. De verhouding tussen Jodendom en Christendom in de eerste eeuwen, Baarn 1979,
'De anti-Joodse prediking van Johannes Chrysostomus' in: **Verkenning en Bezinning**, 19de Jaargang, Nr.2, juni 1985.
Smallwood, Mary, E.,
The Jews under Roman Rule, Leiden 1976.
Stemberger, G.,
De Bijbel en het Christendom, Deel I en II, Haarlem 1979.
Stern, Moritz,
Urkundliche Beiträge über die Stellung der Päpste zu den Juden. Mit Benut- zung des päpstlichen Geheimarchivs zu Rom, **Heft I, II,** Kiel 1895.

Tal, Uriel,
Christians and Jews in Germany, London 1975.
Trachtenberg, Joshua,
The medieval conception of the Jew and its relation to modern antisemitism, Yale 1943.

Vogler, Chantal,
'Les Juifs dans le Codex Theodosien' in: Jacques le Brun,
Les chrétiens devant le fait juif, Paris 1979, 35-75.
Vogt, Judith,
Historien om et image. Antisemitisme og Antizionisme i Karikaturer, Oslo 1978.
Billedet. Som Politisk vaben, Oslo 1988.
Voltaire, Francois, M.A.,
Dictionnaire philosophique, Paris 1756.

Weinrich, Max,
Hitler's Professors. The Part of Scholarship in Germany's crimes against the Jewish People, New York 1946.
Weissmandel, W.M.D.,
Min Hamezar (Memoirs, written in Hebrew), Jerusalem 1960.
Wiesel, Elie,
Un Juif, aujourd'hui, Paris 1977.
Paroles d'étranger: textes, contes et dialogues, Paris 1982.
Wistrich, Rupert,
Der antisemitische Wahn. Von Hitler bis zum heiligen Krieg gegen Israel, München 1987.
Wirth, Louis,
The Ghetto, The University Press of Chicago, 1926/1956.
Wurmbrand, Max and Roth, Cecil,
Das Volk der Juden. 4000 Jahre Kampf ums überleben, Jerusalem 1980.

Ye'or, Bat,
The Dhimmi, London/Toronto 1985.
Yadlin, Rivka,
An Arrogant oppressive spirit. Anti-Zionism as Anti-Judaism in Egypt, Oxford 1989.

Zelensky, Hartmut,
Richard Wagner. Ein deutsches Thema. Eine Dokumentation zur Wirkungsgeschichte Richard Wagners 1876-1976, Wien 1983.

Index

Roman numerals refer to the text on the page in question, italic numerals refer to illustration captions.

List and Source of Illustrations

A number of illustrations has been taken from several books. Detailed information on the consulted literature can be found in the bibliography.

Introduction
Anne Frank Fonds, Basel

The Roman Age and early Christianity
1., 2. Coll. Anne Frank Foundation.
3. from: Meer, Frits van, 1959.
4. from: Narkies, Bezalel, 1974.
5. from: Encyclopaedia Judaica, 1985.
6. from: Blumenkranz, Bernhard, 1965.
7. Rijksmuseum Meermanno-Westreenianum / Museum van het boek, Den Haag.
8. Stadtarchiv Landau Diasammlung, Aufnahme VI/87.

Policy of the Church Fathers and the Early Middle Ages
1. from: Henrikson, Alf, 1980.
2. Bibliothèque Nationale, Paris.
3. from: Meer, Frits van, 1959.
4. from: Kulturabteilung Burgenland, 1978.
5. Koninklijke Bibliotheek, afdeling Handschriften, Den Haag.
6. from: Hirsch, Rudolf, 1988.
7. from: Seiferth, Wolfgang, 1964.
8., 9. from: Kulturabteilung Burgenland, 1978.

The Period of the Crusades
1. from: Eban, Abba, 1964.
2. Bibliothèque Nationale, Paris.
3. from: Blumenkranz, Bernhard, 1965.
4. from: Encyclopaedia Judaica, 1974.
5., 6., 7., 8. from: Rubens, A., 1975.

Anti-Jewish Myths and Legends
1. from: Flaiano, Ennio, 1971.
2. from: Encyclopaedia Judaica, 1974.
3. from: Comay, Joan, 1981.
4. from: Wurmbrand, Max, 1980.
5. Bibliothèque Royale, Bruxelles.
6. from: Ben-Sasson, H.H., 1976.
7. from: Hirsch, Rudolf, 1988.

Economic Sources of Antisemitism
1., 3. from: Eckert, W.P., 1964.
2. from: Wurmbrand, Max, 1980.
4., 5., 6. from: Fuchs, Eduard, 1921.
7., 9. from: Kwiet, K., 1973.
8. from: Rubens, A., 1975.

Towards the End of the Middle Ages
1., 7. from: Kwiet, K., 1973.
2. from: Comay, Joan, 1981.
3. from: Wurmbrand, Max, 1980.
4. Prado, Madrid. Collection Scala, Florence.
5. Museum voor Schone Kunsten, Gent.

6. from: Gielen, J.F., 1931.
8. Kupferstichkabinett, Berlin.
9. from: Jansma, G., 1986.

Reformation and Counter Reformation
1., 4., 8., 9. Coll. Anne Frank Foundation.
2. from: Fuchs, Eduard, 1921.
3. Uffizi, Florence. Collection Scala, Florence.
5. Offentliche Kunstsammlung, Basel.
6. from: Hirsch, Rudolf, 1988.
7. Prado, Madrid. Collection Scala, Florence.

The Enlightenment and the French Revolution
1., 6., 7. from: Fuchs, Eduard, 1921.
2. Bibliotheca Rosenthaliana, Amsterdam.
3. from: Gilbert, Martin, 1977.
4. from: Encyclopaedia Judaica, 1974.
5. from: Cooper, Abraham, 1987.
8. Coll. Anne Frank Foundation.
9. from: Heuberger, Rachel, 1988.

Political Antisemitism in the Nineteenth Century
1., 2., 6., 7., 9. from: Fuchs, Eduard, 1921.
3. from: Kupisch, Karl, 1970.
4. Bild-Archiv der Oesterreichischen Nationalbibliothek, Wien.
5. from: Heuberger, Rachel, 1988.
8. from: Kleeblatt, Norman L., 1987.
10. Collection Josevovitch, Lausanne.

The Racial Doctrine and the Myth about the Jewish Conspiracy
1. BBC Hulton Picture Library, London.
2., 3. from: Zelensky, Hartmut, 1983.
4., 10. from: Fuchs, Eduard, 1921.
5., 6. Coll. Anne Frank Foundation.
7., 8. from: Cohn, Norman, 1967.
9. from: Mackenzie, Norman, 1969.

Nazi Antisemitism
1. from: Kwiet, K., 1973.
2., 6., 10., 13., 14., 15., 16. Coll. Anne Frank Foundation.
3., 4., 5. Wiener Library, London.
7., 8. from: Showalter, Dennis E., 1982.
9. from: Encyclopaedia Judaica, 1974.
11. from: Gummersbach, Hans, 1988.
12. from: Cooper, Abraham, 1987.
17., 18., 19. from: Fritzch, Robert, 1983.

Preparations for the 'Endlösung'
1. from: Heuberger, Rachel, 1988.
2. Israëlitische Kultusgemeinde, Baden-Baden. from: Röhm, Eberhard, 1981.
3., 9. Coll. Anne Frank Foundation.
4. Hauptstaatsarchiv Stuttgart.
5. from: Hahn, Joachim, 1987.
6. from: Keller, Ulrich, 1984.
7. Bildarchiv Abraham Pisarek, Berlin. from: Rosenstrauch, Hazel, 1988.
8. from: Dobroszycki, Lucjan, 1984.

Shoah
ABC-press, Amsterdam.

Postwar Developments in Western Europe
1. Stichting Anlar, foto Jan Vonk, Amsterdam.
2., 3., 4., 7. ANP-foto, Amsterdam.
5., 6., 9. ABC-press, Amsterdam.
8. Foto Bert Verhoeff, Amsterdam.

Antisemitism and Anti-Zionism in the Arab World
1. Collection Z. Schulmann. from: Ye'or, Bat, 1985.
2., 3. Embassy of Israel, Den Haag.
4. Coll. Anne Frank Foundation.
5. from: Almog, Shmuel, 1988.
6. from: Vogt, Judith, 1988.
7., 8. from: Vogt, Judith, 1978
9. Collection CIDI, Den Haag.
10. Collection Simon Wiesenthal Center, Los Angeles.
11. ABC-press, Amsterdam.

The Soviet Union and the Jews
1., 2. 6., 7. from: Cooper, Abraham, 1987.
3., 5. ANP-foto, Amsterdam.
4. from: Vogt, Judith, 1978.
8. Foto Leonid Kelbert, Jerusalem.
9. from: Der Spiegel, nr. 34, 1987.

Denying and Trying to Excuse the Mass Murder of Jews
1., 2., 3., 4., 5., 6., 7., 8. Coll. Anne Frank Foundation.
9. Collection Board of Deputies of British Jews, London.

Coping with the Difficult Past
1. Foto: Vienna report. from: Profil, nr. 8, 1988.
2., 4., 5. ANP-foto, Amsterdam.
3., 7. ABC-press, Amsterdam.
6. Foto: Paul Uccusic. from: Profil, nr. 27, 1987.
8. from: Der Spiegel, 7-7-1986.